Oh FFS!

The Doñana smoker and 199 other twats I'd like to have words with.

Littleoldladywho

Publishing Data

First published 2024 Sliding Scale Books (SSLOLW03)

Plaza De Andalucía 1, Campofrío, 21668, Huelva, Spain.

(c) Copyright Littleoldladywho 2024
Design by Frank Fisher

ISBN 978-84-126023-4-0

All rights reserved

The right of Littleoldladywho to be identified as the author of this work has been asserted in accordance with the Copyright Designs and Patents Act 1988, sections 77 & 78.

No part of this publication may be reproduced, stored in a retrieval system or transmitted in any form or by any means without the prior permission of the publisher and author or her agents.

The publishers and author can accept no legal responsibility for any consequences from the application of information instructions or advice given in this publication.

Dedication.

To my 2 sisters-in-law Sue and Geraldine. One of them keeps any annoyance with the twats in this world in; and the other, who sadly we lost recently after my first writing of this dedication, joyfully let it out in her extremely funny and ahead of its time blog "What Pisses Me Off". I admire both of you!

I'm also lucky enough to have a husband who is so uncomplicated he makes it easier to see the twattishness in everyone else, even though he never points mine out!

Contents

Dedication.	3
On the choice of the word twat.	11
Introduction	13

Twat-speak — 17

- #1 Minor 'twat-speak' offenders. — 17
- #2 Goes without saying. — 17
- #3 Over-loud speakers. — 18
- #4 Exaggeratedly quiet speakers. — 18
- #5 "You always..." — 18
- #6 Interrupters and interruption haters. — 19
- #7 Pretentious corporate-speak. — 20

Conversation twats — 21

- #8 Ageists of all ages. — 21
- #9 Old people telling young people how to be young. — 22
- #10 The pedant. — 22
- #11 He/she who will never admit to being wrong... — 23
- #12 Old know-it-alls... and young know-it-alls. — 25
- #13 Science graduates... and non graduates. — 25
- #14 The 'observable truth'. — 26
- #15 Word police. — 27
- #16 People who get unreasonably upset by swear words. — 30
- #17 Hectoring. — 30
- #18 Grumpy old men/women. — 32
- #19 "FML" moaners. — 32
- #20 'Cultural Appropriation' complainers. — 33

Social media behaviour — 37

- #21 Google avoiders. — 37
- #22 The "Google it!" social media pronouncers. — 37
- #23 Didn't see it or hear it and suddenly know it and share it. — 37
- #24 The Wonder Woman "you are extraordinary" meme poster on social media. — 38
- #25 'Poor me' posters. — 38
- #26 Sympathy drains and label 'owners' (media hogs). — 39
- #27 People who run Facebook groups only for people who agree with them. — 41
- #28 Admins who take themselves too seriously. — 41
- #29 Trolls in the guise of helpful comments. — 42

#30 Overly-positive people.	42
#31 Over-empathetic people on Facebook.	43
#32 "Am I the only one?" on Facebook.	43
#33 Travel braggers.	44
#34 People who holiday in Dubai.	44
#35 'Humble' braggers.	45
#36 Contentment-envy trolling twats.	45
#37 Whataboutist trolls on social media.	45
#38 Empathy-lacking twats.	46
#39 Wellness gurus online.	46
#40 "I'm so excited" interviewers.	46

IT twats   47

#41 Google, Alexa, Siri et al.	47
#42 Mark Zuckerberg.	47
#43 Cookie Monsters.	47
#44 Paywalls on newspapers.	48
#45 Internet troll types who are contrary just for the sake of it.	48
#46 Online only and no customer support.	48
#47 Spanish phone company.	49

Brits abroad   51

#48 Brexitty Expats.	51
#49 Brexpat 'drawbridge raisers'.	52
#50 Brits refusal to learn any of the language of their new home country.	52
#51 British renewable energy protesters in southern Spain.	52

Musicians   55

#52 Singers who never leave a simple end note un-wibbled.	55
#53 Ostentatiously over-breathy singers.	55
#54 Guitar widdlers.	55
#55 Music store showoffs.	56
#56 Over long solos and every musician in the band gets a solo in every song.	56
#57 Musicians who overperform their previously recorded songs when live.	57
#58 Navel gazing musicians.	57
#59 Ugly!	57
#60 Musical 'gatekeepers' (especially the patriarchal ones).	57
#61 All of the BBC musical pun department.	58
#62 Film and television music in general.	58

Fashion twats 59

#63 Fashion cosmetic surgery. 60
#64 Jet black madly arching eyebrows. 60
#65 Facial hair twats. 60
#66 The shorts that are way too short and the bikinis that are actually thongs. 60
#67 Unexpected item in the bagging area. 61
#68 Xmas decoration theme 'huns'. 61
#69 Black polo neck twats. 62

Pet owning twats 63

#70 Twats who get dogs who look mean and then don't take care of them. 63
#71 Heavy metal guitarists who own reptiles. 63
#72 Dog owners who let their dogs roam the streets. 63
#73 Dog owners who say "The more I know about people the more I like dogs". 64

Sport twats 65

#74 Gymnasium showoffs. 65
#75 Jogging. 65
#76 MAMILs- Middle aged men in Lycra. 65
#77 Cyclists in black. 65
#78 Motor bikers who refuse to wear the appropriate gear. 66
#79 Swimming pool twats. 66

Mental and physical health 67

#80 People who say mental health when they mean mental ill-health. 67
#81 "It's my only vice". 67
#82 Lifestyle choices. 67
#83 "Nothing to see here" unusual phenomena deniers. 67
#84 "Eat your food, some people are starving". 69

Medical twats 71

#85 'You must take this fashionable drug'. 71
#86 People who object on principle to alternative remedies. 72
#87 Doctors who get irrationally annoyed. 73
#88 Medical fashions and fads. 74
#89 Both big pharma and big herba-pharma. 76

Emotionally destructive twattery 79

#90 Bullies. 79
#91 Workplace bullying. 79
#92 Those who use the word 'bully' as a trump card. 80

#93 Psychobabbling twats.	*81*
#94 Expecting too much smoothness in life.	*82*
#95 Complaining about favouritism.	*82*
#96 "I've been doing it this way 30 years".	*82*
#97 'Haters'.	*83*
#98 Liars.	*84*
#99 Insult politics.	*85*
#100 Insult arguments and online temper tantrums.	*86*
#101 People who manipulate by pretending to be nice.	*86*
#102 People who demand respect.	*86*

Family and relationships 87

#103 Parents who don't notice just how they speak to their children.	*87*
#104 'Perfect' parents.	*87*
#105 Parents who cave in to their kids' tantrums.	*88*
#106 People who give love conditionally.	*88*
#107 Emotional blackmailers.	*88*
#108 'Nice mummy or daddy'.	*89*
#109 Parents who insist their kids perform in public, or kiss a warty auntie.	*90*
#110 "I'm disappointed in you".	*90*
#111 Negative reframing and teen twattery.	*92*
#112 Popularity manipulating.	*93*
#113 Family comparisons.	*93*

Argumentative twats(and how to cope with them) 95

#114 "Your fault" blamers.	*95*
#115 Defensive twattery.	*96*
#116 Must win the argument!	*98*

Twats in Packs 101

#117 The 'emeritus' Neighbourhood Watch chair.	*101*
#118 The hobby club president.	*101*
#119 Volunteer ill treating twats.	*101*
#120 People who take social crafting too seriously.	*102*
#121 Parents of kids in clubs.	*102*

Driver twats 103

#122 Motorbikers and car drivers who take the silencer off their exhaust.	*103*
#123 Car owners who won't turn the engine off while parked.	*103*
#124 Indicate FFS!	*103*
#125 Over large car for your needs?	*104*

#126 People who tailgate. 104
#127 Car owners who don't appreciate 'small toy joy'. 104

Selfish misbehaving twats 105

#128 Smokers. 105
#129 Twats on buses. 106
#130 Car boot sale idiots. 106
#131 One star rating trolls. 106
#132 Plane seat kickers. 107
#133 People who let off fireworks this century. 107

TV twattery 109

#134 Public figure/celeb twats. 109
#135 Twats who were educated at media school 10-20 years ago editing shows. 109
#136 Stupid section-breaks. 109
#137 Over 100% effort. 110
#138 Backstory stuffing. 110
#139 Advertising twats. 110

Ecology twats 111

#140 People who ignore or sneer at ancient wisdom because it's old. 111
#141 Companies who haven't put any effort into exploring other packaging, 111
#142 People who don't put things in the right recycle bin. 111
#143 Fly tipping. 112
#144 People who believe keeping all animals is bad for the planet. 112
#145 Climate change denier twats. 112
#146 Twatty scientists. 112

Pompous and supercilious twats 115

#147 Medal wearing especially by royals. 115
#148 'Our servicemen' sycophancy. 115
#149 People who think the only source of all truth and all wisdom is Google. 115
#150 People who disagree with everyone else's life choices. 115
#151 Fact checker twats. 116
#152 "I never ask a question unless I know the answer" twats. 116

Bad twattitudes 117

#153 People with more than one 'face'. 117
#154 Those who suck all the air out of a room. 117
#155 Everyone's a critic. 117
#156 Going Dutch. 117
#157 Credit stealers. 117

#158 Not competitive!	118
#159 You're my favourite!	118
#160 "I've got more problems than you" twattery.	118
#161 Those who call positive personal attributes deficiencies.	118

Religious twats — 119

#162 Godbotherers in general.	119
#163 Cardinal kiddyfiddlers.	119
#164 Christian/religious emotional abuse of children.	119
#165 Hellfire twats.	120
#166 People who object to teaching inclusivity in schools.	120
#167 People who call perversion on adult consensual activities.	121
#168 Conservative religious lawmaker twats.	123
#169 The religious right wing in general.	123

Propagandist twats — 125

#170 Twats causing culture wars and pack mentality episodes.	125
#171 Twats who use "Woke, Do Gooder and Leftie" as insults.	125
#172 Envious twats.	126

Sales twats — 129

#173 The twat who trains other people to earn lots of money.	129
#174 Youtube salesmen walking towards the camera.	130
#175 Offers on memberships.	130
#176 Kickbacks.	130
#177 Call centre person to person advertising calls.	130

Scamming and conning twats — 133

#178 Mobility aid scam twats.	133
#179 The gas con twat.	134
#180 Internet scamming twats.	134
#181 The 25 page book twats.	135
#182 Book publishing-con twats.	135

Education twattery — 137

#183 Twats who want to make education boring and inaccessible.	137
#184 Teaching languages through grammar.	137
#185 Teaching maths without physical and visual aids.	137
#186 "Rounded education" twattery.	138

Misogynist, misandrist, narcissistic and psychopathic twats — 139

#187 Ignorant misogynist jokers. — 139
#188 Misogyny enabling twats. — 140
#189 FGM ignorers. — 141
#190 Belittling behaviour twats. — 141
#191 The 'alpha male'. — 142
#192 People who judge everyone's capabilities by the same standards. — 142
#193 People who tell you how you think. — 143
#194 Narcissistic controlling twats. — 143

Identity twats — 145

#195 "You must choose sides" twats. — 145
#196 TERFs. — 146
#197 Dicks. — 150

And finally — 151

#198 Judgementalists twats. — 151
The End... or the beginning. — 152
Biog — 154
Thanks — 155
My other Littleoldladywho books — 156

On the choice of the word twat.

"All the world is a twat save thee and me, and even thou art a little twatty."

(A deliberate misquote. The original attributed to Robert Owen)

The original word in this quotation was 'queer'. Of course it was written when the word queer meant different, strange even perhaps 'neurodivergent'. It only later became an euphemism for anything sexually divergent. In fact it has now been thoroughly 'claimed' by the queer community.

So, of course I wanted to change the word in this quotation to twat. Everyone in the world is some kind of a twat and/or does twatty things from minor misdemeanours to high crimes of assault by twattery. I wanted to write a book about all the different kinds of twat that all of us are. I'm absolutely sure that even people we see as perfectly charming have some kind of twatty behaviour. Maybe 'Saint' David Attenborough is a secret nose picker… well you never know! My husband would say he has a rather twatty voice!

Let me tell you I'm very fond of twats. I am one and indeed, biologically speaking, I have one. I'm very fond of it and also of most of you whose stories and behaviour I include in this book.

The working title of this book was originally 'The Judgementalist' but that wasn't going to rattle people enough to sell any books, and how could I balance writing about how I try not to be judgemental while judging everyone! Well I did, and I have, albeit under a more appropriately inciteful title: or maybe more insightful? I'm just going to gently tease every one of my readers and myself in the hope that you realise I'm teasing humanity as a whole for its unutterable twattyness and praying that we'll all get just a teeny bit more flexible and relaxed for it. If you're still jumping up and down, it could be that you are... a bit of a twat.

For the purpose of this book, the word twat includes all people who have done nothing disturbing at all, who are just mildly self obsessed, or who just make mistakes as to what other people find interesting, fun or acceptable. Then there's the dark side: racists, homophobes, right wing, gammon, gun lobbyists, religious zealots, people who share negative Facebook posts about immigrants etc. alt right Facebook and Twitter trolls. Brexiteers, neoliberals, the mega rich, career politicians, TERFs, holocaust deniers, anti vaxxers, both conspiracy theorists and those who refuse to look at the possibility that there IS in fact a conspiracy, climate change deniers, people who overuse the words "peer reviewed", people who think my backyard has anything to do with them and anyone who is overly triggered by my use of the word twat (although I'm a bit offended myself).

If you find the T word seriously offensive please instead buy the companion books 101 things I've always wanted to say to a dick, and 102 things I always wanted to say to a knob. If all gender-based insults deeply offend you, then this book may be good as gradual immersion therapy. Or you may need to burn it in public, in which case it may not cost too much more than the equivalent in flags and is a lot less toxic.

There are very few twats lurking in these pages who are actually irredeemable dickheads. Now if that term didn't have you jumping up and down as much as 'twats' did, I suggest that you look at your own gender bias. No we don't need to overcompensate, we just need to compensate. I can't stress that enough.

Introduction

I'm old and you could say grumpy. But actually I've recently learned simply to mutter "twat" under my breath, and that release keeps me from being as grumpy as many older people seem to be.

Most of us spend our lives trying to hold back our opinions which aren't always as generous or empathetic underneath as they appear to be on the surface, in order to adapt to our environment. Is that dishonest, or kind? Can it be both?

All any of us really wants in life is love, failing that acceptance and failing that, respect in the form of admiration. We are all teenagers, who are in turn, all two-year-olds just crying out for our needs to be met and our individuality to be recognised and valued. This is the crux of the twat-problem. Most of the twats that we are, is simply a function of us acting-out in order to have some of these needs fulfilled. Those who act in the most twatty ways are the most needy, it seems. So be kind to the twats in your life if at all possible. Because it's also very possible that they are being kind to the twat that you are! Sometimes of course they're simply ignoring it.

I think we stop being such twats when we start to see other people's behaviour or other people's 'type' with good humour and acceptance. To have enough self worth not to be overly defensive. Defensiveness leads to hate when we compare ourselves to other people and decide that we are better than them; especially when we suspect that we might not be.

My generation was taught the anti-bullying trope "Sticks and stones may break my bones but words will never hurt me". But it's simply not true, words do cut, and more often than not, when we are younger they scar, and those scars are the most difficult of all to remove. Bullying doesn't stop in the playground either, even if we pretend it does. I remember telling my 6 or 7 year old son that I myself had been bullied in Girl Guides by the same woman who was, at that point, his teacher. All I could do in this situation was arm him with the knowledge that some adults are simply bad-tempered people and that it wasn't his fault.

If we learn to recognise the bully as having their own issues, they can become a little less fearsome. If we play with words, they can too. In some communities battles with words are raised to an art form. So let's try to be less twatty by admitting the other twat's right to exist and simply give and receive a bit of gentle ribbing gracefully.

We seem never quite to have the wit or repartee to think up exactly the right put-down for a twat who makes us, or tries to make us, feel small in public. So we slink off, maybe cry tears of frustration and injustice. Maybe toss and turn. In the end maybe we decide that twat-revenge is a dish best served cold. This may of course be exactly what I'm doing in this book. Six decades of being twatted upon and too often holding my tongue is about to be released in a huge avalanche of these people and those stories.

I don't consider myself to be a racist, a homophobe, a transphobe, a misogynist nor a radical anything although some may disagree. I am usually called lefty, woke, antifa, but admit I may have a teeny bigoted underbelly that I am working on. Well, I am an old lady after all. I certainly judge people on first sight. I'm not a saint, nor do I aspire to be one. Saints are definitely overrated but I'll get to them later.

Please understand that I'm dealing with people's twatty traits not criticising them for who they are. I recognise that I have many of these traits myself. For example, if I could, I would be a guitar-widdler, rather rich and quite a lot of the gifted or lucky twats within these pages.

Also, expecting people to be a bit twatty somehow releases you from the discomfort of discovering that they are.

You WILL recognise yourself here: probably in several places. Rather than getting really irritated that I've 'got you', try counting the times and patting yourself on the back for being a bigger twat than you thought. Although you'll have to do considerably better than that to get to be President or Prime Minister at the moment.

So, wallow with me in your own grumpiness or get irrationally annoyed at the fact that I've outed you. People are so annoying!

Twat-speak

#1 Minor 'twat-speak' offenders.

People who make double speech marks (air quotes) with their fingers while talking.

People who actually say 'hashtag'.

People who put 'super' in front of an adjective, instead of very: "this ring was super expensive". Ugh. That's taking superlatives the wrong way!

Upward inflection on requests for validation clothed as questions... you know? This comes from American TV and morphed into millennial-speak. My daughter started to do it after watching American teen shows. We could hardly speak until it wore off when she went to university. Or maybe I got more used to it?

And I'm totally going to include 'totally', used in this context.

Australian 'Ahh look'. Just mildly irritating to me, but YH (Young Husband) abhors it.

'Literally!' When it's clearly not. "I literally had kittens". No you didn't!

Argumentative twats on social media who say "so-called" and end their comment with "end of" as if when they say that they have claimed the high ground. You haven't. You have just marked yourself to the world as 100% twat.

#2 Goes without saying.

Talking about what should and shouldn't be said. I'm nominating people who don't understand that a joke has already been made and, thinking *they* have made the connection, loudly make the joke, laughing at themselves as they do it. For example, in a game show True or False section 'the loudest howler monkeys have the smallest testicles' question. The invited celeb made, very loudly, a quite unnecessary joke about the men in her life. An indirect joke made once: funny. The same joke, made twice, loudly and to self congratulatory laughter: cringeworthy.

If you have one of the above habits do try to stamp it out. You don't want people to be giggling at you behind your back because they bought this book before you did, do you?

#3 Over-loud speakers.

I'm afraid this is me. I'm sometimes so loud I can't hear myself think. In England I was one of the loud ones. I'm in Spain now. What a relief to find I'm actually fairly moderate. Maybe being loud is down to believing passionately in something? I think I'm getting quieter as I age... but I am going a bit deaf. What's that you say?

#4 Exaggeratedly quiet speakers.

I find this, and them, a bit unsettling. There's a sort of power shift in over-quietness. It demands attention, feels manipulative.

#5 "You always..."

Starts the twattiest arguments. It's almost never true and so it's one you're going to have to back down from or be proven to be wrong... and you hate being wrong so you continue the argument until that first assertion has been forgotten under a hail of other twattyness on both sides. And we (almost) all do it. If you're itching for a real bust up... start with "You always". That ought to do it.

Want to stop being a twat in arguments? Keep the word 'you' out of disputes altogether and you might never argue at all. Wouldn't that be weird?

#6 Interrupters and interruption haters.

If you hate interruption it's worth realising that your knowledge has sparked someone's thought processes. They may actually be very interested, and keen to show it, often by finishing sentences in their head and then adding the idea they had triggered. I've learned recently that this is a common symptom of a very active brain. Particularly the ADHD brain and is really common in writers and other creatives.

I defend the interrupter. I'm one of them.

It seems common in our over excitable family and I've been told off for interrupting someone in full flow... of an interruption. Two storytellers on the same cruise don't go. Well they do, and they did, but when I thought I was going to have great fun people-watching for twats... I realised that together, both in excitable storytelling mode, my sister and I were the twats. Yes I AM one of those and yes, it IS annoying. But normal for those with creative brains.

On the other hand there is a non-interested interruptor type. I know an older lady who talks endlessly about herself but as soon as anyone else starts to speak she glazes over and "well anyway"... comes out.

Learn to treat interruption kindly and weed out these two from each other. Either you're in the presence of a very interested person who is sparking off what you have to say. Or you're talking to someone who doesn't give a shit. Once you realise which is which you can stop wasting your time being annoyed with the former or attempting to communicate with the latter.

#7 Pretentious corporate-speak.

Using acronyms all the time. Don't do it especially outside of the boardroom. Using two, three and four letter abbreviations all the time is really twatty. Simply parroting the acronyms and other corporate speech of your co-worker tribe makes you sound like a parrot. All speech and no understanding.

Here's an example: "we need to leverage our strategic synergies to maximise our performance", when "we need to do stuff we're good at to make money" would say the same thing without the bullshit. Using leverage as a verb is one example of the detestable corporate bullspeak.

Conversation twats

#8 Ageists of all ages.

Social media post:

"I hate when a 22 year old speaks to me like we're on the same level. Yes, we are both technically adults but you need half-a-dozen real adult heart breaks, some dark bouts with alcoholism, about a decade of depression and a rock bottom before you approach me as an equal"

Bloody hell. Then my ex-husband is on a way higher level than me. He'd be pleased to hear that, as he always assured me he was. I'm not saying that battling a few dark demons doesn't give you any insight, but as an aspirational life choice perhaps not one I'd be pushing on to a generation already weighed down with hopelessness-inducing politics.

If I were feeling my best snarky-self that day I might have replied to this midlife poster: "then when you get to 60-plus you stop being so 'up yourself' and start appreciating the 22 year olds again. You'll have learned yet a little more and will realise that you really are the past, and the world really IS theirs. Then you can start living your best old age and stop being hung up on the disrespect of strangers!"

If you want to get some respect - earn it. It is more likely that an older person will have more experience. When that comes with emotional maturity, it would deserve respect. When it comes with emotional immaturity - quite simply - it doesn't. What's more, you twats are a stain on the rest of our oldie reputations and we other oldies are ashamed to be on the Venn diagram of twattery anywhere near you! So:

#9 Old people telling young people how to be young.

Don't! It's much better if you tell them what it feels like to be old and the crazy things you did when you were young. Leave out only the age-inappropriate stuff. Tell them how many or how few of the things you wanted to do actually got done. Stop trying to right your mistakes through them. Let them listen to your stories (If they want to) and make up their own minds. Start early. Never start telling a teenager what old age means. It's too late (or too early), they aren't interested and it 'will never happen to them'. Start with six or seven year olds and stop at twelve on the dot, unless they ask you. If they do ask you, it probably means you started at six and that they trust your advice on how to get out of a tight spot.

If you don't have any stories to tell, what the hell are you filling their eager little heads with your disappointment for?

Old people are mental health ambassadors. But some of you are pretty shit at it. You have to be able to admit your own stupidity and failings in order to help others to accept their own. If you can't; leave young people well alone and go and work on yourself.

When they start asking you about the bits you left out (this will start to happen in their teens, if you got it right) tell them. If you're very lucky and handle it really well you might just hear those most wonderful of words "Grandma/pa, you're the best!"

Whereas, if you pontificate, you'll just be an irritating old twat.

#10 The pedant.

He never lets a grammar or punctuation error go by without a comment. Come to think of it neither do I. Oh dear I'm afraid I'm going to have to take that one on the cheek too. YH (Young Hubby) says it's common to all of my family and I fear he's right. We are all that kind of twat in my family. It's not attractive though. Not at all. I, as the daughter of someone who used to read "It pays to increase your word power" out of the Reader's Digest at Sunday breakfast must... stop... myself... correcting! Especially as we self edit my book... and doesn't it just show!

#11 He/she who will never admit to being wrong...

Talking of families... not too serious when it's just in the family though, a lot more serious when it's in high places of power. While people who think are often incorrect, people who don't think, will never admit to being wrong.

Be wrong. Being wrong is a step on the way to being correct. Apologising is attractive. Learning is glorious!

People who care passionately often argue. Uncaring people remain placid and often put on an air of friendliness. Those people who settle into an idea, find it hard to be moved, learn or change their minds. What is it about being seen to have once been wrong which so offends our sense of self?

U-turns are good. It shows you have an open mind. Defending the indefensible just makes you a closed minded twat.

In the Spanish Civil war the right prevailed simply by allowing the left to fight among themselves about which form of left was most correct.

Why do we humans defend our erroneous positions so vehemently? Even going so far as to deny the absolutely obvious? What is so very dangerous about saying "I was wrong", or even "I may have been wrong". Even if only a heartbeat after we've stated a position we realise we've made a mistake? Why are people so afraid of vulnerability and error? We see it in our leaders who would rather lie and bluster than show any kind of change in position and we see it in each other. It seems largely to be a male trait, but I might be kidding myself here because I know plenty of women who do it too. Those who would rather unfriend you than admit you might have a point about their racist, misogynistic, transphobic or Brexitty (viz racist) posts for example. We learn that we have to dance around some people whose friendship or whose family-feeling we care about. Feeding the ideas gently. Hoping not to appear confrontational. Accepting the indignity that even if the other person is absolutely 100% erroneous, somehow we have to play the game and make all the moves: in the hope that one day our truth might become assimilated into theirs.

The 'invulnerable' are the weakest of all and yet they get away with our compliance simply by deceit. It must be a human condition because what possibly could it cost us to remove one set of values and say, "Those weren't quite correct" and "I now realise that/believe that" replacing our old position with a new updated set of values. We do it all the time, silently, covertly, shamefacedly. But are we prepared to stand up and admit it? Never!

I am noticing there seems to be a developing narrow mindedness and inability to debate as if once a thought has entered our minds it's impossible to shift. We seem to cultivate this as if having fixed notions and an ability to hang on to the idea that our perceptions of what constitutes a fact can never change, even in the face of all evidence to the contrary. Weirdly, people seem to prefer to defend an indefensible position than ever to admit they were wrong.

And on that subject...

#12 Old know-it-alls... and young know-it-alls.

If you think you don't need to learn anything on any subject, you're wrong. Sharing knowledge is great fun. Don't reject it. Don't be one sided. Give and receive. That's conversation. Why is my song-tourettes giving me "That's entertainment"?

#13 Science graduates... and non graduates.

These are people who know only what they are told at the time they studied and believe that was the peak of scientific knowledge.

"I did a year of a science degree back in the 70s" an educated twat (oh go on; it was my brother) recently said to me, trying to pull his education as his trump card in an argument about whether there really was such a thing as 'Junk DNA'. I pulled out mine: *"and I have a degree in the history of mansplaining and a masters in the half-life of scientific 'facts'."*

Thank goodness for the delay that Facebook gives you to work out these retorts. I'd never have won that one in a face-to-face disagreement. My brother, it has to be said, IS usually correct and often much quicker witted than I. This is another twat point for my brother! Another for me for jumping up and down and dancing at the thought of winning an argument with he-who-is-(almost)always-right. By the way dear brother, I get away with this because it's MY book and I'm a 'winning an argument twat'. There isn't any 'junk'. Mother nature knows better than either of us and is much better than either of us at throwing away the trash.

Graduating in anything seems simply to prove that you can assimilate the knowledge of the time and repeat it back. Bring on your doctorates. Even they don't absolve you from reading up on current scientific knowledge and imagining future revelations.

#14 The 'observable truth'.

(And why some of my most intelligent friends are the twattyest of all).

"There is only one observable truth", one of my most highly educated friends is prone to say from her position of comfortable old age; and of course she is right... all the time. From her point of view, living as she does, on that day of that year in that country with the marvels of the internet and science and the sum of all human knowledge at her fingertips she can only make one set of judgments. The correct ones! If she is unsure she will look at the science. For peer review and for certainty. When she finds it, her existential anxiety quietens and she is certain; until the next insecurity. Her combative style of reasoning has, I'm sure, had her be judged to be in the right many times in her career. If she believes she has a case, she is still fighting it. It makes her feel right: and to be right, in her mind, is everything. And she would never be affected by confirmation bias... oh no!

This group includes people who dismiss as pseudoscience what will never be scientifically evaluated... by the profit makers.

Insisting that "There is only one truth" might seem like mild twattery and a victimless crime, but you will also find many of these in the controlling narcissist category.

My friend observes the truth from one angle and takes admirably scientific measurements and peer review. I look at my peers and the peers of the scientists I'm interested in listening to, and ask myself if they can be bought or, if I feel they are unswayed by financial motivations, whether they are observing the truth from a hill or a valley.

If you believe that we are currently at the peak of human knowledge and have found all the truths there are to be found, then finding the observable truth may take some time but it's pretty easy. You simply weigh the sums of all human knowledge on that subject and pick out the truths that fit your case.

It must be so irritating when a friend comes along and starts talking about phenomena which have never had money spent on their research and who suggests that we are idiots no better placed than trepanners to say what is 'absolute truth'.

The trepanner's observable truth was of course pretty scientific at the time. You do this (cutting a hole in someone's skull), and nine times out of ten you get that result (a relief of pressure on the brain causing symptoms to subside; at least temporarily) but should we blame the firefighter for fires because he's always found at the scene, even though this is an 'observable truth' which is difficult to disagree with. As prof Brian Cox once tickled me by saying in his Mancunian accent "Obvious... But wronggg". More about this in the medical twattishness section.

'Observable truth' believers, please note that from your position, and with vision set to narrow, not all current or future truths can possibly be observed.

#15 Word police.

Let's get over the gender specific noun/adjective subtitle of this book. You know I just use these words throughout it cynically to increase sales don't you? Also for the lovely percussive sound that word makes when you utter it, even under your breath, when someone irritates you. It's like a little can of imaginary negativity repellent.

Over-censoring just leads to fear, loathing and gender/race wars and lets nasty people out of their nasty boxes to spout filthy anti-equality rubbish. I'm not going there.

There's a kind of 'reverse bullying behaviour in playing the "offended" victim however. This gets its own category.

Although we all need to be aware of people's sensitivities and their individual stories, we do need to keep talking and not shut down the conversation because someone well practised in the art of victim behaviour claims the upper hand.

Related to the "word police" is his brother 'the very easily triggered'; and indeed those triggered by the use of the word triggered.

My sensitivity reader quite correctly reminds me that the word triggered is often misused by the alt-right to undermine people's genuine concerns, and suggests I should use the word offended. I'm letting it stay while reminding people that I actually mean 'over-quickly and deliberately offended - as a power play'. The fact that I need a sensitivity reader and that they would pick this out, is because many of the problems here are how words are overused as well as over-censored and, in both ways, weaponised.

The only defence against weaponised words is to disarm them, taking away their power. Giving any of them power over you simply leads to proliferation and 'word wars'.

If you're still angry, or you get angry with me in the following pages, for being on the other side of an argument, you could stop for a moment and just consider the term: "wedge issue". Many of these attention triggering arguments and words have been intentionally whipped up in society and politics just to drive a 'wedge' between people, especially between those with differing culture or belief systems. These divisions don't bring us closer but they do make us more easily manipulated by the Mega-Twats. Take it all in... mull it over and let it go. This is the best way to deal with your personal triggers. People often do it just to get a rise, so if you get a bit immunised by reading this book that can only be a good thing. Overreaction is almost always the wrong reaction.

If you do find yourself getting a bit easily offended, listen to twats. They are the ones who will make you understand the worst excesses of the human condition. Look for the twattyness in yourself because it is there and it is probably indicative of the stuff that's stopping you achieving the very best of yourself. I've been a twat for most of my life and you may certainly argue, all of it.

Don't laugh at twats to their face individually though, only in general satire. Have you ever had an animal that had a sense of pride and didn't like you laughing at it? I have. I had a dog who would snap whenever you laughed at him. And most cats are egotistical twats too.

The older I get the more I realise that even though we are all learning more about each other's mental/emotional states, in a very real sense all the stimuli from social media etc. demand instant and judgemental reactions. So that where we should by rights all be more accepting/understanding, in practise we seem to be less so.

It always pays to be practised in taking a deep breath and asking yourself: what is the other person's motivation? Are they really angry, afraid or just being lighthearted? Are they an idiot, misinformed or being satirical? Are they really bad... or just slightly unhinged by what is going on around them? Of course there are real problem people out there but you can even diffuse their argument by the oxygen of a long breath out and a clear breath back in again.

People who accidentally or deliberately use a word which causes offence are twats of a type, so that's me bang to rights! However, I think we all need to calm our overreactions down a bit. The further we allow our world to go into the blame culture, the nearer we all come to being to blame.

The little arguments about what we should and should not address each other as, may seem important when we feel that we have been slighted or treated as second class by the use of a careless word. Unfortunately winning these little fights has a habit of blinding us to the greater cause and often that cause is a division. A separateness.

#16 People who get unreasonably upset by swear words.

Most of which have very little meaning in other languages.

Americans get really upset by shit and bitch which are mild in the UK whereas Brits think that fanny is a rude word. A Spaniard might call their best friend a c*nt (that's a rare one for me)... Coño Hola! However they are easily upset by the words 'the host' which means absolutely nada to us godless Brits. We use these words like daubs of paint over our speech. I was brought up to think swearing was a lack of vocabulary and the wit to use it. Now I see those extra words as small adornments or great splashes of disrespect, sarcasm or frustration. No wonder it's often called "colourful language".

#17 Hectoring.

People who ask for and then adopt an overbearing tone on your opinion. I have two acquaintances who do this as a matter of course. One is a TERF (see later in the book) and one is decidedly not, but they both want to ask me about and then tell me exactly how to use the words woman, female, girl etc. That sometimes it's not the word that is used but the tone in which it is spoken that is the problem, doesn't seem to figure in the discussion. In both cases the friend wants to 'own' the word. In the first case it mustn't be used for anyone other than her narrow biological interpretation. In the second it must always be used for adults who identify as women. I don't have a problem with giving my honest but careful opinion but I do have a problem when it is wilfully misunderstood or twisted. I find the sort of opinion asking exercise accompanied by overly challenging responses tiring these days. One says "Oh but I thought you were a feminist!". The other "Oh but I thought you said you were an ally?" Both adopting the nose put out of joint surprise-disappointed "Oh!" tone that I learned to brush off when my own mother used it.

I wonder if I ever use it myself. Hmmm.

Hectoring argument is simply a reaction to fear of judgement, an aggressive counter-dominance strategy. If we feel threatened we try to get the upper hand by signalling our correctness under any given circumstance. The more we feel threatened the more strength we gain from our apparent righteousness. Of course there are words and expressions that people find challenging and 'unsafe'. I have every sympathy, especially in these times of social unease, however the line must be drawn somewhere and I always draw it at bullying. I'm afraid my reaction to that is always to do or say exactly what the other person doesn't want to hear. Does that make me a somewhat childish twat? Quite possibly!

Beware people who take on a hectoring tone in conversations in order to steer them in a direction that they have pre-decided. This happens so much these days especially on social media, that it's become a divisive tool in itself. It's often used by the lawyers and intellectuals who have discovered that they can win arguments by aggressive confrontation alone. It's effective. The only defence against these offensive tactics is simply to refuse to engage with them. Most of us however find it really difficult not to do so. It's a skill worth learning and one at which I readily admit I need more practice!

When you do cause actual offence to a twat be prepared to apologise for choosing the wrong language. Learn the art of twat manipulation in the way that people like Louis Theroux have. If you don't understand the art of passive argument, do watch Louis in action. Get the most steps towards rationality you can wring out of them and, most importantly, don't stoop to being a twat yourself.

#18 Grumpy old men/women.

I feel ready to have a much lighter-weight twat next. So let's start with the mild irritations, throwing in a bit of minor twattery we can almost all agree on. If I'm going to 'use what I know' I might as well be upfront about it. I do have a lot of respect for some of the attitudes others would call twattery. I'm going to defend this one. But maybe that's because I'm a grumpy old woman too.

I'm enjoying the rants of grumpy old men, especially those who have a bone-deep truthfulness about them. These people can't be bested because they can never be caught out not being true to themselves.

One of the twattegories that I really want to have a go at are those from the 'couldn't be true to themselves if their life depended on it' category but, funnily enough, the more of a seething pit of dishonest twattitude we see in the world, the more people who really do question themselves to make sure that everything they do and say comes from a good place shine out! The curmudgeon is one of those. There's no badness in their grumpiness. Just honesty.

#19 "FML" moaners.

The lows and highs of having a moan and counting your blessings. Having a moan is a relief, sometimes it's real pleasure. What it certainly is, is a release of pressure, and very healthy too, I think. Think of those stoical friends who never ever moan. Who always show their happy face and who suppress any negativity and carry on to the detriment of their own health, both mental and physical.

On the other hand there are people who never seem to do anything other than moan. My neighbour, for example, rarely has 'a better day' or a 'slight improvement'. Every day she claims to be worse than the day before. I try to keep my patience with her. I really do. After all, she's lonely and in poor health. Sometimes I wonder if she might be in better health and less lonely if she even pretended to have the odd day that was marginally better than the last.

Some people don't know how to have a 'grumbling mildly' bad day. It's all or nothing. On Facebook these lows are often portrayed in the FML (F*ck My Life) message. Or the big brown background with poop all over it. Funny and annoying at the same time. We all need to say 'shit shit shit' out loud even if only visually. Personally I'm not fond of the FML message because it seems pretty rude to those who are about to lose theirs. I understand that life seems unfair to you at times but the 'poor me' mentality really doesn't help anyone. There is a reason wellness coaches tell you to practise gratitude. Otherwise, what a waste of every precious day wishing you had a better one. Spend some time looking around.

If you want to have higher highs you may have to accept having lower lows and since you can't always just hold your breath because you're on a high, or hold it all in when you're on a low. My advice to my friends, my kids and all my readers too, I suppose, is to breathe out. A nice long sigh. Both physically and mentally. If you want to count your blessings and shout out your happiness to the world please feel free. We all need to and enjoy doing that sometimes. But equally remember to have an occasional moan. That's what your friends are for and we don't any of us have the perfect life or the perfect natural selfie-pout.

#20 'Cultural Appropriation' complainers.

This whole cultural appropriation thing is an unnecessary minefield. A very large part of our current music and our musical heritage would simply have to be destroyed because of its roots in the blues. And then the blues itself would have to be destroyed because of its roots in slavery and plantation songs. All art is theft, or rather all art is derived from the beauty of other art which we admire. We all have to acknowledge our influences and the beauty of the originals we base it on. I'm not religious but there are people who may well insist that I shouldn't make polymer clay flowers, as that's originally god's work. In fact there are religious groups who would say just that. Let's continue to show respect for the artists who came before us and just make beautiful art which celebrates all of our cultures, each in whatever way we are moved to make or perform it. And let's not allow people with a hidden agenda to drive us.

Of course people get annoyed when they see badly performed hakas and badly made dreamcatchers. I find it a bit irritating to hear white men 'jolly up' blues music too. We used to joke about 'the blues solicitor' singing "I'm broke and I'm hungry". In the end it all morphs into something different as it has done throughout the history of man. The roots are still the roots but the branches are often grafted. Most educated people can work out which is which and for the rest, does it really matter if it makes them happy?

Possibly the most ridiculous story of cultural appropriation twattery I ever heard was last year.

Facebook crafter friend's experience:

"Over the years I've been accused of many things but "Typical cis-male cultural appropriation of gay iconography" was a new one.

The reason? We have the temerity to call our business "Rainbownames" and we didn't have the name he wanted in the rainbow design."

If anything, we are being set up to be deliberately and vacuously culturally divisive on this subject. You can almost see Steve Bannon directing a posse towards calling cultural appropriation on everything just to rile people up against each other. This is definitely a political wedge issue.

Enjoy exploring cultures, making that dream catcher or sewing that native American outfit or learning plantation songs.

Social media behaviour

#21 Google avoiders.

People who ask on Facebook things like "what time is the next train from South Romford?" Rather than look it up themselves on the same device they're already using! There's an excellent reply to these types... in the form of this link Let Me Google That For You.

https://letmegooglethat.com/

Thanks to Lucy for this one.

#22 The "Google it!" social media pronouncers.

The ones who, when you question the source of their information simply say "Google it". If you can't actually cite your sources then your information has no validity no matter how many times you say "The information is out there... find it".

Want to make a pronouncement without being a twat? Be prepared to back it up if challenged; or get your coat. Use the link above if you're in a hurry.

#23 Didn't see it or hear it and suddenly know it and share it.

I don't have any examples of this to share but we all know someone who just likes to be in every conversation as THE expert. Especially if it's a gossipy judgemental thread.

While we're on judgemental people, have you noticed that people who tell you not to be judgemental are often the most judgemental of all. I have to admit I'm both of these twats. I am both judgemental and I smile saccharine sweetly, and tell people not to be so judgemental while judging them as arses. I know a few people like me, too... Arses!

#24 The Wonder Woman "you are extraordinary" meme poster on social media.

I know they mean well, posting this on international women's day, but some days it's difficult enough to maintain the energy of just being ordinary. And, if it's difficult for me with my lucky genes and my extraordinary parents, I know it must be difficult for others. Do we have to have pictures of wonder women in all sizes and colours and in wheelchairs to make us feel like maybe we could be / should be aspiring to more?

Can we just be good enough mothers and can we just wear 'trackies' and no make up and be suffering from menopausal sweating?

And can we let our ideal man have an average size penis, a battered car, and fart occasionally?

Sometimes the pressure to be extraordinary is worse than the pressure to conform. Can we sometimes just be enough?

#25 'Poor me' posters.

Trauma tape loops. I know some people do need a hug or a hand out of a situation from time to time. I'm not talking about the clinically depressed, but the validation addicts.

The greatest of these are 'addicted to sympathy' posters. These are the same people who suck all the air out of a room and all the positivity out of a situation! They will typically post comments like 'why are you being so harsh?' and 'I can't say anything right' and 'why is everybody getting at me'. Even when people are being helpful. They will request agreement that someone else has been unfair to them and will pick on every positive comment as a negative. Applying confirmation bias to everything and trying to garner agreement and sympathy that everyone else is being so horrible. They will get it too, from another sympathy addict; who will expect it in return.

I do sympathise with these people because they have unmet needs, but I'm not sure the endless replay of sympathy garnering posts will solve their serious problems and I would like to see them get the help they need. Unfortunately the feedback they get is feeding the avoidance of recognising that there are some problems they need to solve; and some they need to let go. I really don't want to minimise their pain though and I hope they get out of thinking this alone will solve them. And that's why this group and the group below go together into a self-fulfilling pain cycle.

I'm not going to give you a snarky response to these people as they really are needy. Handle them gently but set firm boundaries which they may or may not appreciate immediately but will respect in the long term.

#26 Sympathy drains and label 'owners' (media hogs).

The race to the bottom of problems and to the top of sympathy in social media etc. One of the most demanding people I've ever met happened to be blind and female and mixed race. I had plenty of empathy for her problems but very little for her twattishness. If people squeeze the very life out of you by demanding more and more sympathy because they deserve it more than you, it really stretches tolerance to snapping-point. Having more problems does not give you a free be-a-twat pass. On the other hand this girl did have more to cope with than most. How do we get along with people who are a bit 'fighty' because they have had to be?

Of course there are some really serious piles of problems people have to cope with but sometimes it's really difficult to find the victims under the victim mentality. And how do we find the strength and the right way to say no to someone who is throwing their 'underweight' about?

Why is it that people cling on to a label and want to own it so strongly and exclusively? I recently saw a post where autism was mentioned and one person said "we are all on the spectrum to some degree". And she's right. Although some are on it at the opposite end. That's what a spectrum is. It's all the colours and even those ends where there doesn't appear to be colour at all. And yet someone jumped down her throat for saying this and claimed she was minimising the problem and even asked her whether she had been diagnosed, or was a doctor.

Some people who are on the autistic or ADHD spectrum don't actually want a diagnosis and are happy just recognising that they are normal too. Real live-and-let-live behaviour would not be to get all twittery about someone saying that 'we are all on the spectrum'. It's a figure of speech which is not belittling. She's trying to say that we are all normal no matter to what extent autistic-like traits affect us. It's time those who preached inclusivity actually included other people with other levels of mountains to climb, and stopped saying "my problems are more important than yours".

I did have a nice, positive conversation very recently with a lady who really didn't like the word neurodivergent and asked why people used such an abusive word. The lady is diagnosed autistic. She does sometimes come over as combative in her posts but our conversation revealed why. She likes to pin down the meaning of words really firmly. I suggested that neurodivergent was an umbrella term and really useful for people like me who have never been diagnosed but were clearly on the edge of one possibly more interconnecting spectrums (or is that spectra?). She suggested that if I didn't want/get a diagnosis maybe I shouldn't be using the word. Well, I wasn't using it, as such, just explaining why I *might*. Then she suggested in my case I might use "abnormal" instead. She wasn't being rude, she was just trying to get to the crux of the label problem. We actually had a nice social media conversation on this subject but often these discussions can get toxic because people feel like their safe space is being attacked.

Once again we don't know other peoples stories; people will always have more to cope with than you can possibly imagine. But there are also a few who not only speak up, but amplify only their own stories. So if we have nothing to give we're best staying out of these conversations. Intersectionality throws up a whole range of twattishness on all 'sides'.

#27 People who run Facebook groups only for people who agree with them.

These admins range from the narcissistic to the needy. You will get members but you'll only keep sycophants and those who play your game just to use you. These people might do well to learn to accept a challenge or two. Learn the art of discourse. Gatekeeping people out because they might be more interesting than you only shows your insecurity and is not good karma. Staying out of these groups is the best option.

#28 Admins who take themselves too seriously.

I was once refused admission to a humour group. One of the entry questions asked why I wanted to join the group. I said because all the admins had different-coloured hair and I noticed they didn't have blue yet. I was out. No sense of humour!

#29 Trolls in the guise of helpful comments.

"I'm struggling to find a nice way of saying this" comments. Followed by an unnecessary and vitriolic flame. These are not even well disguised as helpful. Clearly you didn't struggle very hard.

"You shouldn't do this on this group" followed by a 'bigging up the group' comment. These are posters who probably want to be admins or moderators, but aren't. I'm ashamed to admit I've done this myself and so I'm a twat. Refer this transgression to the admins.

Also people who say "not being funny" meaning "I want to arm myself against you saying that I am insulting you". Almost always followed by an insult.

#30 Overly-positive people.

On social media, sometimes happy people can be annoying to me. Why? Because that much happiness looks unbalanced and therefore contrived. Even though I'm a pretty positive person myself.

We hear a lot these days about counting your blessings. Some of our friends put up happy Facebook messages with "feeling blessed" icons and pretty pink and purple backgrounds to tell us how good their lives are. Sometimes we are moved to look at our own lives in a more positive sense but more often I find them irritatingly smug. Although on the other hand I truly believe that having a positive attitude towards things really does make life better. But we have to suspect that there's a darker flip side to these people and that behind closed doors they cry. Or that all this suppression of the negative might pop out somewhere else.

So, now I've had a go at the overly positive and the overly negative, let's see who else I can annoy!

#31 Over-empathetic people on Facebook.

"You OK hun?" I don't buy it. As soon as the word 'hun' comes out I wince. This might be unfair as 'hun' is now a commonly used friendship word. Is this person really 'beloved'? EEK. I'm clearly a behind-the-times twat for finding this irritating rather than accepting it as a common and current use of language. Sometimes it feels as contrived and as shallow as "thoughts and prayers" from an NRA club member.

#32 "Am I the only one?" on Facebook.

The Facebook poster stay-at-home mum *"Am I the only one who vacuums daily, changes the sheets twice a week and irons everything except underpants?"* My first answer was almost kind... I said something along the lines of *"You say you are 'woke' I'd be asleep after all that but do what makes you feel good. Personally I have no truck with ironing."*

The judgementalist in me is jumping up and down for several hours afterwards. Not sure whether I should have said *"Yes love... get a life"* or *"haven't you heard of climate change (all that electricity and washing powder FFS)?"* The nicer me realises this is a self-validation exercise.

Then Mrs Judgemental (me) wants to pair with Mrs Nice stay-at-home mum to provide a slightly passive aggressive snarky answer, replying with a question. A better question would be: *"am I the only one who cares about the answer to this question?"*

We are all looking for meaning to our lives and you seem to have found yours. But are you trying to find your place in the hierarchy of perfect women? I'm both fascinated and annoyed that this is still a thing. I'd love to have a twice a day vacuumed house. So I bought a robot. Still can't be arsed to set him off more than a couple of times a week even though I do have 2 fluff-monsters and a garden and no

Homes and Gardens boot scraper... should I be aspiring to one of those, hun?

"Am I the only person never to have shopped at Primark?" Sounds like "I would never lower myself. I can afford to shop at proper shops". *"Am I the only one never to have watched Love Island?"* Honestly I'm judgemental about these programmes too but normally not twatty enough to put it in the form of a social media sneer. If I did reply to this minor twattery with a sneer of my own it would probably be *"It's your choice how you validate yourself"*.

#33 Travel braggers.

"Look at all these wonderful places we go!" The only people who don't get this twat point are those who don't get to travel. Award yourself a point for every new place you've bragged about and double if you bang on about the same destination every single year.

These are the 'addicted to recognition' twats. These people constantly want you to see them and compare your humdrum life to theirs. I'm not talking about marketing here, I'm talking about dinner photos, slimming photos, wine photos, pictures of their feet at the pool, the cocktails they're having tonight, desperate for a click or a like. Oh dear. I think I've just 'twatted' one of my dearest friends!

#34 People who holiday in Dubai.

I'm grateful to a relative for this one, which I hadn't thought of. I wasn't sure I fully understood her or my own feelings on this one at first, but I was sure people who holiday in Dubai are some sort of twat. More recently she told me it was about people who claim to be LGBTQ allies but regularly choose a holiday in Dubai where it is illegal to be gay. I have another reason for including this twattegory. If you really must holiday in Dubai, please don't take your 'battery operated boyfriend'. I have a relative who did just that and now has a police record in Dubai for importation of lewd materials! She said she wouldn't have minded so much, but it was a really 'posh' one that her husband bought her.

#35 'Humble' braggers.

"I'm so humbled by this award y'all gave me so I'm going to splash it all over social media." For this read "I need my ego boosted on a regular basis. Tell me again how wonderful I am" with a side order of "what a nice normal person... unaffected by fame". You aren't humbled. Your ego has been fed. What you are is vaguely embarrassed about how much you enjoy it. Go ahead and enjoy it. You probably even earned it. Say thank you. It's better. Don't tell those that voted for you that they made a mistake. This is more over-nice twattery.

#36 Contentment-envy trolling twats.

I've realised that one of the major causes of online twattery is contentment envy. People can't bear to see others more content than themselves. This gives rise to the "royal scapegoating" twat. They quite like royalty as long as they look royally miserable, but woe-betide any that are happy. Those who tell you where you're going wrong in life, if you are content with what you have, are just envious and want you to join them in their misery.

#37 Whataboutist trolls on social media.

We've all met/conversed with these. They bring up a totally unrelated incident to prove that what you're talking about isn't important. These people tend towards self importance and IMO very much worth muting, at least.

#38 Empathy-lacking twats.

I'm talking about those who believe that you should just shut up and get off their conscience. Those masters of emotional detachment won't even talk about let alone fight for a just cause because they believe that they are more hard done to than anyone else in the world.

#39 Wellness gurus online.

Generally mostly unwell themselves. What makes them forgivable or even laudable is that they are finding out what has made them unwell and are trying to help others out of their holes. Unfortunately a lot of them are a wee bit dishonest about how far they've come.

Here's a pretty hard and fast rule. If your 'guru' admits to, even embraces still being on the journey themselves that's a big tick. If they speak down to you in very hushed tones... they're probably a twat.

#40 "I'm so excited" interviewers.

Interviewers who say this on podcasts and videos, but who are so clearly not. Don't do it. It's so cheesy it's even worse than "awesome". You clearly didn't listen to the poor guest's response as it wasn't 'awesome' at all it was just mildly interesting but you wouldn't know that. If you are going to try and ramp up the excitement you'd damn well better sound vaguely interested!

IT twats

#41 Google, Alexa, Siri et al.

I'm in a stand/piss-off with my Google nest. Every time it feeds me a "and now for a pause" annoyance because it can't get advertising enough, trying to irritate me into paying for its premium services, I give it feedback. I told it several times in several ways where it was going wrong in life, eventually distilling it down to "stop being a dick" which it pretended not to understand. It's a simple system, though, and can't take long jokes at its own expense. This could be my excuse to learn to get very 'pithy' indeed.

#42 Mark Zuckerberg.

I can't stop myself from nominating this one. BTW when did Zuckerberg stop looking young and innocently confused, and start looking creepy? Maybe that's when Meta arrived. Maybe Meta is what made me think this way. It's simply awful, especially if you are juggling small multiple income stream micro-businesses (yes, I am). I wonder how those weird narcissistic types juggle several relationships at once when I can't even handle more than one Facebook entity without swearing and having to open several different tabs to switch between. I have no secrets but do have more than one Facebook public face.

#43 Cookie Monsters.

(With apologies to the 'real' cookie monster).

Accept cookies? Polite but artful and confusing style and positioning to force you to accept accidentally. I politely decline and find a way to turn off... or back out.

You *must* accept cookies... or we'll give you a page you didn't ask for and don't want instead. I find myself shouting "f*** off!" at the computer screen.

No I don't want your goddamn cookies especially when you put "your privacy is important to us" followed by a deliberately confusing path to reject. Unless you can deliver me an actual chewy cookie right now, at no cost, GO AWAY!

#44 Paywalls on newspapers.

Even on the one I actually pay into gives me annoying messages at the end of every article. "You can't have forgotten that I give you three whole quid every month!" But putting The Daily Sh!t behind a paywall!! At least it keeps people like me from exploding on a daily basis. Another F off with an added invective: *"I didn't want to see the wretched slime spewing out of your nasty little rag anyway"*. Don't drag us into your wall. Give or don't give.

#45 Internet troll types who are contrary just for the sake of it.

I asked a question about what books or childhood experiences might influence those of us who decided to live off-grid. The troll hops on and says (paraphrased) "It's not books... things just happen".

Some people are "things happen to me" people and some are "I make things happen" people. I think what influenced us along the way made a difference to our decisions. Then of course other shit does just happen along the way. But mostly we're in the driving seat even if the roads are a bit slippery at times.

These people's ability to challenge and to hold a contrarian view on every subject can be quite impressive.

#46 Online only and no customer support.

All businesses that only have an online presence and do not answer customer enquiries.

#47 Spanish phone company.

This gets a last minute twatting for insisting we could only report our phone problem after connecting - with the phone that isn't working!

Brits abroad

I have a high disregard for expats... but of course not 'expats like me', oh no. I'll say it's because I learned the language, I don't get drunk and red faced and swear a lot. Actually I do swear a lot. More so the older I get. Perhaps swearing a lot is just an old age release of inhibition or maybe I too am an expat twat.

#48 Brexitty Expats.

Although Spain is a bit more resistant to/slower in the growth of racism, it still exists. One lady told a story on Facebook about being abused on the phone when asking if a non-EU directive about paying for visitation permits applied to us. Unfortunately "why should we be any different" is true. On the other hand, it's sad that she met one who was prepared to voice it in an abusive manner.

Our 'lovely' Brexitty friends in Britain were just the petri-dish for a cancerous growth in 'othering' everyone. It happens here too. It's all part of the plan to make us all look somewhere else to place blame for our problems than where it properly rests. Right at the top and when I say top... that shouldn't imply esteem. This is why I get so annoyed when I hear expats here crowing over others who are in a less stable financial state than themselves. It behoves us to understand where all this shit comes from, and take care of each other.

"Europe needs them more than they need Europe" apparently. Ahh well it is currently coming back to bite them. They are realising that freedom of movement, or not, applies to them because now they are the immigrants.

#49 Brexpat 'drawbridge raisers'.

I was a member of an Anti-Brexit Spanish expat group where, once Brexit was definite, I started to see comments along the lines of "If you haven't got your paperwork sorted out yet, you deserve all you get". No eccentric stories were tolerated. No longer was this a group of people with disparate hopes and dreams but they reverted to the selfishness of the tribe where you were either in (and that seemed to be white middle class retirees) or out of that group. I was always going to be out. Their politics was never my politics. Their politics was always any party that got them 'remain' so they could stay in the lifestyle that their previous Tory voting had got them. For one glorious moment it seemed like the machinations of the neoliberals were beginning to become clear to them; but the window of enlightenment closed when their individual rights were assured and they started to creep back to an 'us and them' group.

#50 Brits refusal to learn any of the language of their new home country.

This is because, they say, English is a universal language. They find it difficult, most people on the Costas speak English anyway, they only need a beer. Then they complain if they get poor service.

#51 British renewable energy protesters in southern Spain.

Understandable. Who wants an enormous energy mega park in their beautiful backyard? However renewables are better than all of the possible alternatives. It would help their argument if Spain wasn't a net importer of energy. One of the problems here is that of these protesters some won't see the connection between energy needs and their poorly insulated air-conditioned houses.

Also their argument that it will use a lot of water is flawed since cleaning uses very little water indeed and if plants are grown under the shade of the panels they can have a double benefit for both that land and those plants. It may even be somewhat less ugly than the hideous plastic greenhouses, and more productive.

If they really don't want these constructions, making it unprofitable for the big corporations to build huge solar generating plants must be part of the answer. On an individual basis most people can do something towards that by generating their own power, or part of it. Thus not needing to buy so much of their product. Choosing to have traditional style Andalusian homes with high thermal mass would help instead of the badly insulated conurbations. I do understand that not everyone can afford solar, but campaigning for support with individual solar could ease the need for large plants.

Certain crops including bee-friendly plants are failing because the daily temperatures are simply too high and the plants would do better in the partial shade of solar panels placed so that all the agriculture can go on around them. Runoff from the cleaning water can be used to water the crops as can collected rainwater. Spain can be a renewable paradise with just a little investment and a lot of open minded thinking.

The idea that Andalusians should work to standard European hours is pure idiocy on the energy front too. I live there and it's impossible to work from 2 in the afternoon without air conditioning between June and the end of August. Air conditioning isn't very eco friendly.

So if you want to protest solar farms, make sure you back it up with alternatives. I would say that sense beats nonsense... but I'm afraid when mega profit is involved you have to have a very good argument to take down their machine. A more efficient way of changing the need for even more electricity is simply not to use so much of it yourself.

Musicians

I'm afraid twattyness abounds in the music industry, from teenage angst through mid life crises to those who hoped they died before they got old but then refused to do the decent thing; or at least recant.

#52 Singers who never leave a simple end note un-wibbled.

Otherwise known in our house as 'Whitneying'.

#53 Ostentatiously over-breathy singers.

How sexy am I? I must have been great, I'm so out of breath.

#54 Guitar widdlers.

Arrogant dicks. Stop pulling it on stage. We've seen it before and it's not that big or clever.

The problem with being a guitar 'ace' means that you will only appeal to the part of the demographic that is interested in the battle. They want to watch your 'licks' and see if they are as good as you and imagine they are better. If you want to appeal to the part of the listeners that want to feel the emotion, you should put that and not clever posturing into your music. Whichever you choose you should certainly remember what you're doing and make sure you remember to keep it fresh. Remember how you were feeling when you wrote the song and make sure you are feeling it whenever you play. Or at least 'act'. Performing is not about how clever you are, it's about how you make the audience feel. This may be sour grapes because I'm not a good enough guitarist to 'widdle'. Or 'shred'. And no, I don't want to shred. It's public onanism.

Which brings me to the:

#55 Music store showoffs.

I recently upbraided an online and video selling musician who I actually rather like and respect, for putting this advert out:

"What never to do at a music store – or in your solos."

I won't print the whole ad but the crux of his mail was the "you can sound better when showing off in a music store" one.

Teaching people that really twatty way of being, in music stores, is what's wrong with the music world and what keeps women out of it. If you go into a music shop, you're there to buy an instrument, not to show off. What the hell does it matter what other people think of your playing? In fact I find that kind of dick swinging behaviour a real irritation, and it's a bit off-putting for women to walk into a guitar shop and find it happening. At the risk of confirming gender stereotypes, usually the guy behind the counter will hand the bloke customers a guitar to play (show off on). If it's a lone girl, he, or the other clients will show her how well they play it instead. C'mon! Don't be part of the problem that makes music all about how big your musical dick is! Let people, especially women, walk into a guitar shop without seeing all those dicks on show!

#56 Over long solos and every musician in the band gets a solo in every song.

Just NO. One verse/segment/sequence a set is enough. And one musical showoff each song is enough too. Maybe 2 if you really have something to say! If it runs to three musicians or one musician doing three verses he (because it's almost always a 'he') should have his arms broken when he comes off stage (according to Young Husband). And yes, I do secretly agree. Just because you can, doesn't mean you should. It's all a bit predictable. I want to be surprised. Just a few days ago I was listening to a really clever piece of music with an unusual beat. I pointed this out to YH and said how good I thought the drummer was. Then he went all showoff and did not one but 6 entire verses of solo. Ugh. What had been delightful became tedious, in the space of just a couple of minutes. Leave them wanting more for goodness sake.

#57 Musicians who overperform their previously recorded songs when live.

They lose their emotional timing in an attempt to be better, more interesting or more "Jazz" than the album. It's the equivalent of writers who over describe. Leave us some space for us to feel... please!

#58 Navel gazing musicians.

How pretentious. The audience is more important than your muse. You're in the entertainment business! You want to be profound. Go stand looking deep with your finger on your forehead in an art gallery.

#59 Ugly!

While we're on guitarists, I'm giving a twat number for pulling ugly faces while playing guitar. I'm going to leave this un-criticised though. I think it is hard to concentrate on a tricky but moving piece without putting some kind of sex-face on! However, if you're also widdling or shredding or putting in another unnecessary solo and making faces to look profound... you can have double twat points.

#60 Musical 'gatekeepers' (especially the patriarchal ones).

These are the musicians that either knowingly or unconsciously keep other musicians down by not telling them about gigs, not telling venues about them. This is usually people who are in some way insecure about their own position in the musical 'hierarchy' and they'd rather crush a potential musical success than be part of its encouragement. I've met two of these in my life. The first one was in my hometown. Recently I've been avoiding the feeling that I've come across another gatekeeper. But you know, you get a sense when someone is insecure. If it looks like gatekeeping and feels like gatekeeping... then it's probably that. It's pathetic. Don't let your own lack of confidence allow a gatekeeper to stop you from achieving your best. And don't be part of the problem. Just don't, especially if you're a woman... with a guitar.

#61 All of the BBC musical pun department.

Especially for morning programmes. And even more especially Homes Under The Hammer. This was an endless stream of cringey musical puns. Very few of them were very clever links. We can all Google song lyrics with certain words in. They got paid for that?

#62 Film and television music in general.

It's too loud and insistent and spoils enjoyment of the story. Just because you can, doesn't mean you should. Your part of the production isn't the most important. Anyway it doesn't work in most people's living rooms. I know my lovely brother has worked with and likes him, but personally I can't bear Hans Zimmer's film music. Clever... but over demanding.

Fashion twats

Yes it's all a matter of taste and culture and actually It's a love hate relationship I have with fashion. I'm so glad it exists. I really enjoyed experimenting with it myself. Statements must be made. The art that is fashion, is glorious and affirming but sometimes looks pretty stupid from afar. I have been and am a bit of a fashion twat. The slightly anarchistic sort. After all, I'm heading for seventy and insist on having blue hair. Not the pretty old-lady pale blue rinse of my grandma's era. But the "how old does she think she is?" and "It's blue... don't like it... tough!" blue.

Fashions are constantly changing and you WILL look back in your old photographs and ask yourself when did you ever think that was a good look. Some of the stupid foot (30cm) high hairstyle and similarly wide shoulder pads in the 80s as well as the minimising the rear end "does my bum look big in this" thing. Then the pants down under the arse cheeks. This is all completely eclipsed by fake tans, ludicrous boob jobs, lip fills, bottom implants and unnecessary surgeries. Facial, body and pubic hair is in... out... in...out.

A simple note on this, from a little old lady to the young would be: if you don't want to look old when you're 50 don't fix your fashion to any physical changes such as tattoos or facial surgery/facial piercings. It might look cute while it's in fashion but when it goes out of fashion or even if it comes back you'll look as out of fashion as a 60 year old with a mullet! So, IMO, the whole fashion industry are twattish

My current pet hates, though, are:

#63 Fashion cosmetic surgery.

Those who prey on people, often in their teens, who feel they would be more acceptable ergo happy, if only their lips and breasts were fuller or their cheekbones were higher or, for goodness sake, their labia were the same (short) length. Do not have this surgery if you ever want to give birth. Those stretchy wrinkles are there for a reason! Lip-fills look awful... yes they do.

#64 Jet black madly arching eyebrows.

This is irrational of course because it doesn't damage anything or anyone. I could more reasonably have chosen to hate permanent destruction like stretched piercings, tongues cut into two, full body tattoos. But no, I choose to highlight these over-painted eyebrows which remind me of theatrical dames, the Joker, Humpty Dumpty and haunted dolls and so... they scare the shit out of me.

#65 Facial hair twats.

Over-long beards, over wide beards, straggly beards. Beards that are tightly trimmed into one thin line, or plaited into a string... ditto moustaches. Beards with no moustache... moustaches with no beard. The single pretentious triangle between the bottom lip and the chin. Some of my very best friends choose twatty facial hair styles.

#66 The shorts that are way too short and the bikinis that are actually thongs.

I admit I'm envious of all those pert tanned bottoms and I think women should be able to wear what they want but don't tell me it's not about sex.

If you don't want old ladies telling you what is appropriate for you to wear, you better damn well not mind us sporting our floppy boobs on the beach or having our nipples on show under a T shirt or wearing our shorts too short. If visualising any of those make you say NOOOOO! then ask yourself why. If the answer contains the word sex or 'disgust' and when broken down the disgust is about inappropriate age to look sexy, then you have to admit that that's what flaunting those bits is about and that *you* feel it's inappropriate for older people to be doing that. That's fine. That *is* the way most people feel. I just don't want to hear "It's not about looking sexy it's about making me feel good". *Yeah right. It's about making you feel good... looking sexy.*

#67 Unexpected item in the bagging area.

Men who complain about having to wear something under their short shorts to stop it all hanging out. Stop whinging for a moment and think about the hoops women have to jump through not to be judged. See above. If you really want total freedom you have to allow it in others without either judging or groping. Can't promise that? Thought not. *"Put it away then, there's a good chap!"*

#68 Xmas decoration theme 'huns'.

"Ooh no we can't have that green bauble... this year we're going silver and blue hun!" I have to admit to a mild version of this. Mine is very simple. I refuse to buy any gold or yellow or blue for my tree. But to be fair that's been my rule forever and wouldn't stop me putting an antique bauble that my parents bought or something sweet that my grandkids made on our tree. I used to be a no-plastic-at-all (real tree only) person but I relented one year when I realised how far those trees had to come. Although personally I do think growing trees for Xmas trees is not actually that unsustainable, as long as there is land to grow trees and new trees are grown and that they are carried on boats rather than aircraft.

#69 Black polo neck twats.

Steve Jobs, Elizabeth Holmes, and a very dear friend of mine called Pat. Mild minimalist-pretentious fashion twattery. I don't have any excuse for finding this unreasonably annoying.

Pet owning twats

I've come to the conclusion that dog people are different to cat people in that dog people expect compliance. Cat people are content enough with a world they can't control.

#70 Twats who get dogs who look mean and then don't take care of them.

Your dogs bark everywhere, growl everywhere and you never take them for a walk but just let them out on the street even though they are on the dangerous breeds list. Typically your dogs have names of heavyweight boxers or well known criminals.

Owning a dog is a good thing if you really care for it. If you just "want one to look good" forget it because you'll get bored and mistreat it and your neighbours. Yes you will.

#71 Heavy metal guitarists who own reptiles.

That hasn't been cool since the early 70s and even then was only weirdly cool to young teenage girls. Yes, my first boyfriend Mick the chick-magnet had a baby boa constrictor which he accidentally flushed down the toilet... twat!

#72 Dog owners who let their dogs roam the streets.

And of course those who don't pick up their dog's mess. In our street they all lie and say they do pick up after their dogs. Those are the ones they simply let out to shit where they want. They don't follow them with a scoop and they don't clean up if their dog makes his mess in front of your house because that's safely round the corner. And then they look at you as if you're the thoughtless unreasonable one if you point it out. Grrr!

#73 Dog owners who say "The more I know about people the more I like dogs".

That's because humans just can't get along with you. You aren't likeable. You aren't empathetic. Dogs wouldn't like you either if they understood the shit you talked. They know which side their bread is buttered though. You may be a control freak but you are (usually) a reliable food dispenser.

Sport twats

#74 Gymnasium showoffs.

They start a year long expensive contract because they can't be bothered to walk to work. They probably have a dog they don't walk either. They are injured on their first day because they want to look like they know what they're doing and want instant results instead of working up to it slowly. This guy (sorry not really sorry, it IS usually testosterone fuelled) starts on day one with all the gear, over trains and is knackered by the second session. The third session never comes.

#75 Jogging.

Jogging isn't good for you. Walk or run for goodness sake. Jogging is very high impact for very low benefit. Yeah I'm going to piss off half my relatives with this one but don't come crying to me when your knees are broken at the age of 55. Ah well yes my knees will be broken by then too but I'll be a great deal older.

#76 MAMILs- Middle Aged Men In Lycra.

If you aren't actually training and checking your times, put something sensible on that doesn't wear your nipples off. So what if it means a bit more drag? That will just make you work a little harder. Then when competing, you'll be even fitter. You look silly... yes you do! Everyone says so.

#77 Cyclists in black.

Especially those who don't have lights. You want to die? Your choice. You want to cause an accident that kills someone else? That is probably jailable. Think about your clothing choice for a millisecond!

#78 Motor bikers who refuse to wear the appropriate gear.

I was at the scene of an accident where two boys very nearly died because they were riding around in the sunny weather with their helmets undone and wearing shorts and tee shirts. Aww the joys of youth! They suddenly found themselves flying through the air and having a one sided argument with a vicious lamppost. Spoiled my afternoon and my leather jacket, and didn't do much for their next year or two.

#79 Swimming pool twats.

(Subgroup of teenage twats) Live and let swim! Bombing people who have limited vision, limited lung capacity or just a fear of being bombed is not funny. Take your sad bereft little lives to the other end of the pool and have some real fun instead. Or grow up to be one of the other sort of twats in this book. Your choice. Twattery starts young.

Oh and kids watch out for the other sort. Flattered by the attention of an older swimmer hanging out on the side of the pool? Don't be. Those are the creepy twats your mother warned you about. I was 16 and my sister 14 when we very briefly met one of those. You don't realise... at first. Fortunately that was the the closest brush (ugh) I ever had with one of that type of... No, twat is too mild a word but I'm not going to bandy the P word around more than necessary. That's another fave of the far-right.

Mental and physical health

#80 People who say mental health when they mean mental ill-health.

To say "I have mental health" is confusing. I had mental ill-health in the past. Currently I have mental health.

#81 "It's my only vice".

Dieters who don't realise that "It's my only vice" probably means it's the one thing you have to give up on. Or "I can't stand plain water." Err yes you can, and it will probably help!

#82 Lifestyle choices.

Some of the saddest twats of all are those who try to disguise their mental ill health as 'influence'. They pretend to espouse a lifestyle in which they give up on pleasures they can't have anyway. I'm thinking of the dominating social media hard-man who thinks people who enjoy food or cooking are "wusses". Also the social media cleric who didn't have to give up anything that is available to him and who is as far from the "judge not" teachings as you can get. This behaviour surely won't age very well.

#83 "Nothing to see here" unusual phenomena deniers.

There are people who are not prepared even to look into unusual but oft-reported phenomena. They simply 'don't believe', and that's that. Personally I don't believe in every weird and wonderful claim, but there are a few things I'm prepared to be open minded to and some I'd love to see scientifically investigated. One of these is the idea that everything has a vibration level. My brother (a musical scientist) was questioning this idea. I explained to him the idea of healer types trying to smooth out vibrations as (potentially) like degaussing a screen. Yeah I guess that's a 1980s computer geek expression. Something that because of his age he understands but most readers will not. Old screens (pre-LED and liquid crystal) had a habit of getting a bit mashed in their displays. They had to be regularly degaussed of their wavelengths... smoothed by correcting or removing a magnetic disturbance. Now I might be talking complete bo***cks here too, but just maybe there are fields that get a bit messed up affecting our 'vibrations' which in turn affect our biorhythms. And if any man tries to explain to me that biorhythms don't exist I'll hit him with a large piece of cotton wool pad soaked in light blue liquid, and let him work out my meaning... and his own stupidity.

A friend of mine claims to see auras. And I'm not prepared to rule that out. In fact recently I asked her if maybe it could be some form of synaesthesia which I do believe in and in fact I have. I am able to perceive colours in many other ways than just visually and often the reverse. A song can have a colour for example.

Researchers in Spain have found that many of the individuals claiming to see the aura of people - traditionally called "healers" or "quacks" do actually present the neuropsychological phenomenon known as synesthesia (specifically, emotional synesthesia). Then there's sexual synesthesia which I can't help but imagine is quite common... If you see images or hear music or see colours during sexual activity, maybe you have it too.

I don't see auras. However I do get bad feelings about people and very good feelings about others and it often transpires that I wasn't wrong. Maybe that's just unconscious reading of micro expressions.

#84 "Eat your food, some people are starving".

Yesterday. That's the yesterday before I first wrote this of course... not your yesterday, when you're reading. I know that didn't really need clearing up but editing is weird! Anyway, yesterday I didn't eat all of my meal and I moaned "Oh no, I don't think I can eat all this!" to my husband who is the rather excellent chef of the house. "Well never mind" said the lovely husband "nobody's going to tell you off". And that was true. And that is another reason why I'm comfortable with this man, and that is why even though at times I lose my rag at his laid back-ness, I strive to be more like him. Because you see he's more than half way to that innocent who has no fear. We can tell our well-fed children that it doesn't matter if they eat or don't eat the thing we bring them at lunch time. Four hours later there will be more. No argument, no panic, no uncertainty, no fear and definitely no manipulation. If there's ever a real need to 'clear their plates' we will all know about it!

Since I wrote this probably a half million more children in the UK are actually in poverty and many are going without adequate nutrition. Don't overstuff your kids. Do give a dozen eggs to a needy family. You bought too many... right?

Medical twats

I love the medical profession and they saved my life but some medical knowledge that should be questioned, isn't. For reasons that often have to do with profit or the status quo.

#85 'You must take this fashionable drug'.

It's often positively frowned on to avoid drugs. I've often gone against doctors advice and had eyes rolled as if I were a no hoper and it was my own fault if... blah blah. "Ativan is non addictive" 'they' said. "Doubling your Lansoprazole after 20 years of use will cure your reflux". "Statins will stop you from having a heart attack or stroke"..."You need to get rid of your cholesterol".

Disclaimer: I am not a medic and some medics will disagree. Time and science will tell.

In all 3 cases I've gone against my doctors decision to prescribe or to over-prescribe.

Drugs are often used to treat symptoms that would tell you a different story if you listened to them. We are so afraid of saying no to doctors! For example statin over-prescribing.

We've been treating cholesterol as the worst of the bad guys for decades. Seeing the fact that it's always on the scene of inflammation as if it caused it. Some medics say statins "radically improve health and lower the risk of heart attack or stroke". Backwards logic and not necessarily true. In fact the presence of cholesterol in the system is a signal that something else is wrong. You will find cholesterol at the scene of inflammation just as you will find firefighters at the scene of a fire. Inflammation is the real problem and you should not mask the symptoms. And yet there are still medics doing this rather than looking for the cause which may well evolve into something more major while hunting down and killing the firefighter!

Just this week I saw a slight change in tone but which *still* implies that cholesterol is the bad guy. So here's a half twat-point for the people who nearly got it right but said on a health site… "Oats reduce cholesterol. The first marker in heart disease" and don't realise what that second sentence actually means. Cholesterol is the 'marker' because it appears as a result of inflammation. It would be better to say "Oats reduce inflammation, which, incidentally, causes an increase in the body's production of inflammation-battling cholesterol. Reducing inflammation reduces the amount of apparent cholesterol which the body produces to fight it". Or simply "Oats appear to have an anti-inflammatory effect".

#86 People who object on principle to alternative remedies.

Most medical breakthroughs come from ancient 'alternative' remedies. To say these haven't been peer reviewed is actually a fundamental misunderstanding of the real meaning of the term. Many of these remedies have been more thoroughly peer reviewed, over aeons, than our new pharmaceutical wonder drugs. I'm not trying to say that all alternative remedies are good but there are some financial advantages to denying the usefulness of cheaper alternatives.

While we're on this one…

According to two separate and both intelligent friends (one of them a pharmacist for goodness sake!), nutritional and all ancient medicine is "pseudoscience". They forget that the foundations of medicine are in ancient 'science' and that actually being centuries old and having survived the stupid fads and fashions does not give it less credibility, but rather, more.

Take a look at an ancient apothecary list and you will see chemicals and herbs which are still used today albeit today they are packaged in bubble plastic and silver foil and have big pharmaceutical companies names on them. I was prescribed bicarbonate of soda pills by my urologist. They cost 7 euros for a month's dose and a side order of a load of plastic waste. A teaspoon and a tub of bicarb is less than a tenth the price and almost zero waste.

I'm really too bored to repeat here all the medicines that have been used and are still being used for common complaints. All the herbs and foods which support all the body's functions with macro and micro nutrients. I was sneeringly told there is no need to support liver function by helping it to cleanse the system because *"we're not a dirty toilet"*, according to one natural-health denier. Except that, in a very real sense, we are exactly that. If our toxin cleansing system fails from our lymphatic system to our liver and kidneys we are in a very bad place. We need to be regularly cleaned and there are food-state medicines which are well known to help with those functions.

Medical companies are now falling over themselves to create immunological drugs which have existed in nature forever. And where are they looking for them? In nature.

Do doctors still take the hippocratic oath? Hippocrates, the father of modern medical science said *"Let food be thy medicine and medicine be thy food"*. Honestly, I haven't heard a better nor a more sensible pronouncement on health.

#87 Doctors who get irrationally annoyed by any patient questioning their judgement.

Everyone should question everything. Not rudely. But a good doctor should listen to their patients especially if their patient has more experience of their particular diagnostic problems. For the last several months I've been trying to tell my doctor that *every single one* of my urine tests *will* come back as contaminated, as I have an ostomy, if she doesn't inform the lab what we are checking for. I keep trying to explain that it's precisely the difference between the regular contaminants of ostomised patients' urine, (vegetable cells from the wafer, intestinal mucosa from the piece of intestine that comprises the diversion etc.) and anything that is unusual, like candida for example, I want to know about. This doctor can't get past the word 'contaminated', because she has little experience of urostomies. And the local lab doesn't know to look further. She insisted on explaining to this little old lady exactly where candida is 'normally' found. As if I didn't know!

#88 Medical fashions and fads.

More medical opinion twattery, subject to the half life of facts. Medical 'facts' (assertions) of the past now either questionable or throughly disproved (of course my assertions may be wrong too because I'm a self-confessed opinionated twat).

Here are a selection of the things we were once told one thing about, but that opinion has changed over the years.

"Fat is wrong." "Ultra low fat diets are good for you." "Taking fat out of yoghurt and replacing it with sugar is better for you." All these were commonly held beliefs in the 80s and 90s. All disproved.

A group of Danish scientists investigated why the French don't seem to suffer from cardiovascular disease as much as their high saturated fat diets would suggest. The researchers looked to diet to explain this so-called French Paradox. What do the French eat a lot of? Cheese. I'm not sure what conclusions they drew but I would say, if asked, fat intake doesn't store in dangerous places in the body. Sugars, particularly fructose, are converted to fat by the (over-worked) liver and wrap around the organs.

"Salt is bad for you." Only half the story. Actually if you lower your salt levels too far that can be even worse. In hot countries you need more salt. If you don't eat meat you need at least a little added salt.

"Tobacco is good for you." Yes, they really did say that in the 40s and 50s!

"Cannabis is bad for you, good for you, bad for you." When a pharmacist saw the two drugs prescribed for chemo nausea and nerve damage he said I'd be better off with cannabis. The same pharmacist who told me alternative remedies were pseudoscience!

"Chocolate is good bad good bad good." Ach who cares! I've had cigarettes and whiskey and smokers and drinkers in my life. Chocoholics are much more fun.

"Red wine is good bad good bad good." I'm no scientist, but after a limited trial the results are in. A glass of Rioja makes me feel pretty good. Two make me feel pretty bad.

Coffee... ditto.

High carb diets... good bad good bad.

Low carb... bad good bad good.

"Herbal medicine is 'alternative' and new fangled." Actually herbal medicine is the original medicine and it's modern drugs which are alternative.

"Long periods of exercise every day are good for you." This used to be the accepted wisdom. Now research is starting to show that shorter periods of more intense exercise is better.

Well I know the real answer to all this is that moderation is good for you... except that I'm sure too much moderation is also detrimental to your mental health!

A little of what you fancy certainly always has and always will do you good!

"*Antibiotics: you must take the full course*" is now under question.

#89 Both big pharma and big herba-pharma.

We see what you're doing. This is how they get the results they want... and they call it 'science'.

If you want to be a successful pharmaceutical company twat this is what you do:

Pay for tests. If you don't hit the jackpot with that test, tweak the parameters of the test until you hit the gold dust result. Then bury the original test results. Easy.

Medical/scientific opinion. Gather opinions from qualified people that agree with your assertion and discard those that don't. Simple.

Side effects. Adjust results to find people that benefited during the trial and call this "empirical evidence".

Put down all data that doesn't agree with you as "anecdotal". Drop the word "evidence". Make sure you don't let the public know that it doesn't suit your case and that's why you don't accept it.

Empirical. Accepted - read as 'science'.

Anecdotal. Rejected - meant to be "read as nonsense non-science" or even better use the word "pseudoscience" completely to undermine its quality.

It's worth saying that you can apply either of the above words to reported effects.

Deliberately refuse to do testing on easily accessible remedies. Unless they can be concentrated into something you can charge more for. Then prove the benefits of only that 'strength'.

Withhold all evidence of the best way of using 'naturceuticals'. AS IF only your formula has the precise balance required. (Turmeric works only with black pepper.) While removing information about potentially dangerous side effects of the concentrates and/or pharmaceutical equivalents.

Don't give the patients any clear method of reporting side effects. In other words, don't collect negative data.

You don't have to be a conspiracy theorist to see that 'science' can be manipulated at least where it relates to what data you choose to collect and what you choose to reject. Lies, damned lies and statistics.

Emotionally destructive twattery

#90 Bullies.

Bullies are twats of the highest order. But there is a possibility that the bully themself is the damaged one. It is possible to immunise yourself against bullies as an adult, but it's not easy especially if the bully is also a narcissist who is a black belt in the dark arts of gaslighting and DARVO techniques. Bullying is way too big a subject for this book and if you are suffering from it I don't want to make light of or belittle experiences that can be extremely damaging. There are lots of books on these subjects. If you are being persistently bullied at work, for example, I recommend you read some or follow some Youtube videos on those subjects. It's playground politics. Afraid the other person might be right? Call them names. And get your friends to call them names too. Now you have a gang. You're still wrong… but you feel safer. The only way to counter bullies is to ignore the names or, if you can, defuse them.

#91 Workplace bullying.

I never wanted to go out to work (so I almost never did). I can't handle office politics. People who are envious of you will try to scupper you and you don't know who they are because you may have actually f***ed up or it may be someone just playing with your self esteem. It's still bullying even as an adult. But just like kids in the playground, those of us who are oversensitive are more likely to take it on and allow it to hurt us. Your best defence is a can of imaginary negativity repellent in the pocket. If someone starts trying to bring you down just imagine yourself taking it out of your pocket and spraying it at them. Then smile. Thank them for their advice and walk away. Try to drop your judging/fear of judgement. Then it's more difficult for anyone to bully you.

#92 Those who use the word 'bully' as a trump card.

When do the gentle arts of sarcasm and the noble art of satire become bullying?... I think they don't. You can't have an individual episode of bullying, you can only have collective bullying or repetitive acts that come together as bullying. One person saying one thing doesn't make a bully. So if I say something out of order and I will, probably several times in this book, for goodness sake don't agree with me, get behind me or start jeering at other people, because all I want to do is poke gentle fun where I think it needs to be poked. It's the getting together to mess with someone's head that becomes bullying.

All your 'spaces' are safe from me. If I get near to the knuckle or close to the bone as they say it's just because you have a vulnerability that you're hiding and you might need to be more comfortable with, so that we can stop polarising into combative tribes.

I think discussion might help. I think going back into being allowed gently to take the piss without going too far. A little more allowing ourselves to be seen as individuals with opinions and a little more tolerance of those opinions. Open discourse is not helped by hate speech but neither is it helped by thought-policing. Getting the balance right is the hardest thing we'll ever have to do but we must do it. Being OK in ourselves, is the first step. This will never come from parenting too strictly or too carefully. We have to be able to bang our knees in playground debates and yet know where the boundaries are. We have to support the more vulnerable. We have to be able to be wrong and we have to be able to gently show people their errors. Since piling on to a mistake is bullying in itself.

When the 'bully' card has been played it really should be pointed out. Then you can hit the rewind button and aim for a more constructive exchange.

#93 Psychobabbling twats.

People who have learned a few psychological terms and bandy them about, in order to devalue what you're saying. Recognise these manipulation techniques as they are very controlling. They make me wonder whether they've had too much therapy themselves... or maybe too little. In many cases they are actually reflecting their problems onto you. I was once in a long(ish) term relationship with a very intelligent... psychobabbler.

Words they may use: 'projecting', 'passive aggressive', 'deflector', 'inauthentic'. It seems to have become a thing in certain jobs to learn a bit of this language as a contemptuous dismissal technique. It can be really difficult to work out who is the victim and who is the perpetrator when these kinds of power plays happen in the workplace or in family dynamics. Most people don't even see these 'darts' coming and the one using the psychobabble is rarely the real victim in these exchanges.

The angry side of me wants to counter this by psychoanalysing these people right back, but it's counterproductive. My husband gave me a good line (he doesn't get as rattled as I do) he says to me "you only have the truth".

Sometimes you just have to close these sort of non-productive discussions down. Another close down line I discovered, quite by accident is "I don't need fixing". Because often these uncomfortable encounters come from people who do love you but want you to be more biddable or more like their idealistic idea of you. They think if only you would listen to them your life would be happier. And, looked at more kindly, they perhaps feel somewhat responsible for your happiness. You have to let them know. They aren't.

#94 Expecting too much smoothness in life.

In your day, your employee, your moods/mental health, your parenting. You can't have ups without downs. Do you really want to smooth off the sparks of brilliance for something as tawdry and forgettable as consistency? We all strive for contentment but it's here already. Contentment is when you can find something to be grateful for every day including the ups and downs. And yet most people would use the expression "ups and downs" to mean the problems of life rather than the joys.

#95 Complaining about favouritism.

When I asked my granddaughter what her earliest memory was, it wasn't the consistent loving care given to her by her other grandma. It was the unusual visit to my house. Unfair... but true. As I got older when my parents lived near me it always seemed that it was the distant children who were the favourites. Then they moved to live near one of their sons and I'm sure he'd report that we were then the favourites. The appeal of the unusual is very strong.

#96 "I've been doing it this way 30 years".

Usually in response to a good idea you've had. I met one in my early days as an author. We were doing something new at the time (step-by-step digital photography which never left the digital domain until it was printed as a book). Quite groundbreaking at the time, but just the way things are done now. This type finds new tech threatens their superiority in the field. Remember this old has-been, probably once was at the top of the game. Handle them gently but firmly. Try to massage their fragile ego by thanking them for their many years of knowledge and for helping you get this far. But be firm with your "*I just want to try this because I believe it will make 'our' work even better"*. Then put something in the pot when their inevitable leaving-do comes up.

Now I'm the one who has been doing things a certain way for 30+ years, so I need to look to my laurels!

#97 'Haters'.

We have to find out what the mistakes that the Baby Boomers and Gen X made that made us all so horribly polarised into haters. I think it has to do with emotional flexibility. We must be allowed to change our minds. We must be allowed to make mistakes and to confess sins. There isn't one of us who hasn't made a misinformed comment at some time in our lives. There are also very few of us who haven't shared a post which turned out not to be true or which was part of the mass manipulation. I did, and I think it was my brother who pointed it out. Once you realise what you've done or said... ooh cringe! Who among us hasn't felt happier being on the winning side? Why then is it that we allow such deeply flawed individuals to lead us while policing our neighbours for small transgressions as if our lives depended on it?

Our leaders were supposed to be beyond reproach. Of course very few of them were, but at least that is what we looked for. We don't need superhuman neighbours, and then twats for leaders. It really should be the other way around.

Now, it seems we are all not only hunting for labels to stick on ourselves, we're hunting for pejorative labels to stick on each other.

Many of the labels we stick on other people don't stem from a place of understanding, nor of love, but of envy. I've stopped being understanding of envy; if I ever was. If you want something, go for it. If it's not so important in your life that you won't go for it... you didn't really want it. This is probably why I'm more creative than rich. I'm noticing more and more that the haters seem also to be either envious... or projecting.

#98 Liars.

Some people are liars. A lot of people are liars. In fact I'd say most of us fib from time to time. I know I do. But there's an honesty to yourself that some people do and others don't have.

A little homily I was taught as a child that has served me well all my life is "To thine own self be true, and it will follow as the night does the day, thou canst not then be false to any man". Of course it's incredibly archaic and needs modernising. It would be difficult to make it more succinct because it embodies a very multifaceted idea of being 'true'. From being an out-and-out liar; to omitting truth; through fibbing to make life easy or interesting. Having a belief in your own value is part of being true to yourself.

Have you noticed that some people look too good to be true? They probably aren't all they would like to be.

Then there are those who can fib at you but there will always be the twinkle in their eye because they know and they know that you know, that what they're saying is in some way embellished. These people irritate the real liars because they don't understand why they are so relaxed in the face of whatever is slung at them.

If you know deep inside yourself that what you've done or said is true and honest to yourself you have the relaxation borne of knowing you can never be caught in a lie. That's a precious thing and that alone makes this homily worth updating. If you can't be honest to yourself you're going to get caught. The worst liars of all are those who find it easy to lie about tiny unimportant things even in the face of overwhelming evidence, rather than apologise for something. Do they really think the respect we have for them is in some way augmented by this rather than damaged? Do they think we can't see through these little 'wasted' lies?

There are some people who are out and out liars. And I know one. I don't know whether to feel sorry for this one or call them a twat, because it looks like they also have Munchausen's syndrome (not the by proxy version or I'd have to be a lot more vocal about it). This type just lies and gathers sympathy all over social media. And they are so believable you can't call them out on it because it makes you look like the bad guy. Outing one of these practised liars if they are at work or in the same business as you, is a courageous or foolhardy game to get into. I know some who have been burned by trying. This happens a lot in political reporting too... but that would be another book.

#99 Insult politics.

There's so much of this around at the moment and it always says more about the insulter than the person the insult is aimed at. Online keep an imaginary can of negativity repellent at hand. The person who tells you to "grow up" is usually the most immature. This one, who recently replied when I suggested that calling people idiots is not the best debating tactic, with no sense of irony, told me "Learn not to lecture others. I will do as I feel. You've got a bloody cheek. I don't need your posturing. Grow up!" This one calls herself a therapist. I really feel the need for an emoji here but 'proper writers' don't use emojis, so I guess I'd better leave it there.

#100 Insult arguments and online temper tantrums.

People who seek to put themselves in a powerful position by making the other person's reply somehow appear worthless by using reductive language about their qualifications to have and express an opinion.

Tantrums don't work for those who aren't actually narcissists. They just reveal themselves as a little spoiled. You don't really need to worry about these twats as they throw their point into the bin with their temper tantrum. The ones you really need to worry about are the efficient narcissist gaslighters (see narcissists). If you don't know what gaslighting is it's very well worth looking it up along with DARVO.

#101 People who manipulate by pretending to be nice.

We all know at least one of these, often in the workplace or in family groups, includes passive-aggressive 'niceness' "I'm nice, why isn't he/she?"

#102 People who demand respect.

By demanding it, they lose it. If you demand respect it may be because you need it but you won't get it because you behave in ways that disrespect others by not considering that they have a point of view or their own needs too. This is unintentional twattery practised by those with the most need and the least likelihood of getting their needs fulfilled. I have a lot of sympathy but not a lot of hope for these people. They are difficult to deal with as co-workers and difficult to keep as friends because the nearer you get the more they want your respect and since they don't know how to earn it... they demand it.

Family and relationships

#103 Parents who don't notice just how they speak to their children.

I wonder if that's all of us? I once heard a tape recording of myself directing my eldest son to help me at changing time with his baby brother. Ugh! I was awful. Really demanding. I think all parents should tape record themselves and note their conversational style when under pressure. Before forgiving themselves for being normal good-enough parents, that is.

Oh the beauty of innocence! Children are also beautiful and endlessly fascinating when they make mistakes based upon how their parents speak and reflect their parents' twattery back at them. I can't ever forget when my son came out with "Don't arg-me!" What a cute and innocent way of showing me how I speak to him. Another twat point for me, I think.

#104 'Perfect' parents.

Yes there are parents who are just too good. They strive to do everything perfectly... much better than their own parents. The only problem is that kids who never graze their knees on the realities of life, who can't look after themselves or make their own decisions... are the most deprived of all. Too much parenting can be as bad as too little.

I was once a volunteer on an anxiety helpline, chatting with a suicidal girl. She told me she'd been in care. But explained that her problems weren't what most people would fear about the care system. She had been so well cared for and protected that when she reached the age of 18 and was thrown out into the real world... she was totally unprepared. She said that in a way she would have preferred it if things had been a little more challenging for her. I hope there was a long term happy ending. When I first spoke with her she was terribly afraid of doing some exams the next day. I persuaded her that it didn't matter if she passed or failed, she would feel much better when they were over. We spoke a year later and she'd done the exams and passed!

#105 Parents who cave in to their kids' tantrums.

You are making a horrible human being! You'll suffer first, but then we all will... and so will they. Subgroups 'I want' and sub group 'won't eat' and subgroup 'sulkers', all twats in their own right. You are not a better parent if your child is quiet because you've given it so much chocolate it's now stunned by a sugar coma or nauseous. Don't give it a handful of bangers so it can go and terrorise the neighbours and leave you in peace either. It's not being a good parent or neighbour. The kid is now a twat, and so are you.

#106 People who give love conditionally.

They don't always know they are doing it. They are just accustomed to that form of interaction and manipulation and may have suffered it themselves. It's a sad cycle. You have to have empathy for the victim but the perpetrator is damaged too. Once you realise you will never get their unconditional love, you can start to realise you don't need it.

#107 Emotional blackmailers.

These are people who want you to act differently and are prepared to throw poison critical darts at you in the hope that it will force you to make a different decision or apologise to them to make them feel more in control. Ignore emotional blackmail. Nothing good ever comes of bowing to it. Just remember that sometimes those who are using it don't realise it and really just desperately want a different outcome. Often it's in the family and practised between loved ones using passive aggression and victim behaviour.

Don't cave in to it, but sometimes it's worth explaining why you won't be doing what they want.

My mother had very few annoying traits. She was truly loving, creative and inspirational. She did have a chocolate hiding habit and a 'Hyacinth Bucket' telephone voice, which we always laughed at. She also had a teeny bit of manipulative victim behaviour, which I recognise runs in the family. Her put-out "Oh" is the stuff of family legend. I had a conversation with her once, over the washing up. She had tried-on the 'victim thing'. I don't remember that part exactly but, unusually, I replied to it this time "You can't do that anymore". She asked why. I said "because you're dead". It was a rare moment of lucidity... and catharsis in a dream.

#108 'Nice mummy or daddy'.

Step parent twats. I have some sympathy for them because I recognise it's born out of insecurity. Usually the new wife is trying to outdo the old wife by being extra kind and accepting. Also the over-nice stepdad trying to out-cool the real dad.

This can often be an emotional manipulation game with the children as pawns or just insecurity because of the legendary step-parent-as-evil narrative.

Fortunately it comes to an end eventually when the new step parent gets bored with the 'toy' son or daughter or has a few of his/her own. But before that, this twat double damages the child by ruining their original relationship and then rejecting in favour of the new toys. It also causes years out in the unpopular parent wilderness for those original parents strong enough to hold their ground, which isn't easy.

Co-parenting takes some serious self discipline not to let any new partner skew the relationships or change the rules, whether you are the new or the old parent. Any parent who takes the easy road instead of proper co-parenting is definitely a parent twat.

#109 Parents who insist their kids perform in public, or kiss a warty auntie.

Don't do it. It's abusive to tell your kid they have to perform an act that makes them feel uncomfortable. Definitely not a good beginning for self determination and resistance to invasion of their private space.

#110 "I'm disappointed in you".

Q: What is the heaviest thing in the world?

A: The weight of parental disapproval.

There are a handful of 'weapons' in relationships that you should never use. If you do, you really risk breaking the relationship, and this is one word which can do just that.

Parents who make their children shoulder the burden of their disappointment can feel they are helping by steering the child in the right direction. Unfortunately disappointment is emotionally destructive

Usually parents make this mistake but it can be siblings, relatives or friends. This twat decides to express 'disappointment' in someone else, and in doing so has thrown away the benefits of acceptance. The benefit of acceptance is that you can learn from the other person. Even if you disagree with what they are saying or what they are doing on a fundamental level you can learn why they react to certain situations one way, or another. If you express your disappointment you cut off all lines of learning.

You expected a person to be this way or that and they aren't and you are disappointed. Maybe you are disappointed that they don't simply come round to your way of thinking. Because, it seems to you that they ought to, because you are a friend, a parent, an expert. And they are your friend, your child, your sibling or your subordinate. Often there is more to be learned from the person who doesn't simply agree with you to keep the peace and yet you have simply decided to close the conversation because you are disappointed in the response.

You will remain disappointed and what's more, if your disappointment is due to an argument, you have not won or lost an argument, you have simply taken the worst of it away with you. With neither agreement (bonus) nor agreement to disagree (keeping the channels of communication open). You may have inflicted a wound on the other person in the discussion especially if that person is your child. These wounds can leave deep scars which are difficult to get over. The disappointed often have their own disappointment wounds. If the person trying to pass on this sentiment is a fully functioning adult, you may simply shrug and say. This person can never be happy until they drop this way of interacting.

One of my friends is disappointed in me. "*I thought you were a Marxist and a feminist and now I find you're not. I'm extremely disappointed*" she says to me over a cup of chamomile tea, forgetting for a moment that I have neither confirmed nor denied being either of those things. I have just been my usual un-pigeonhole-able self, which seems to frustrate her inordinately. I reply with some kind of waffly but probably over smug dismissal which I'm sure irritates her even more. This is the way we have always been. She, trying to lead me to her point of view; and I, equally certain that whatever it is I'm sure that it's no place I would ever want to be. I think we are each other's nemesis. Her, ruled by parental rules and regulations and me, having drawn a happily medium-to-long straw on that life lottery, not being at all interested in pinning my colours to any mast or being tied down.

Actually, in spite of the differences in our life path, we are both similar in that we are trying in some way to prove ourselves worthy. I have to accept that it's both kindness and need that drives her judgement.

If someone has used the disappointment 'cudgel' on you, you could try remembering that their parents may have used it on them and it's not your fault that you can't heal that.

#111 Negative reframing and teen twattery.

A very smart friend of mine once said to me, "you know, kids make stuff up? You have to tell them". I'm forever grateful to Marie (RIP) for this. We were probably talking about the problems of being responsible parents to troubled teen or young adult kids at the time. Problems on both sides which are so difficult to resolve without great experience. And where do you get the experience from? We all still feel the weight of the mistakes in our own parents' efforts, and vow to be better parents ourselves, that is, until we've made an equal number of mistakes ourselves by which time it's often too late.

I was thinking about my son and his lovely kids, my grandchildren of course. I was specifically thinking about us talking about cold showers in this heat, how we'd agreed they were healthy. My son told me he was getting the kids to switch to cold at the end of a shower, no doubt thinking of the very real health benefits and possibly of Wim Hof. This was a game of course. As a good dad my son wants to introduce his kids to as many healthy habits as possible.

Suddenly it occurred to me how kids negatively reframe caring parental actions when they reach teenage and have an audience, and angry hormones. I started to feel uncomfortable. Just imagine the conversation. "My dad used to make me take cold showers". "Oh no... what a beast!" Suddenly the love and the health benefits are gone and the new memories, backed up by the listener's horror, are of an uncaring father. Unfortunately that new re-framing can stick harder than the original squeals of delight and feelings of accomplishment when the kids get to 10 seconds then 20. Even if they earned a hot chocolate. That hot chocolate wouldn't earn the horror of their friends... when angry at the world, a 'bad-dad' story will do nicely.

We, so-called 'adults' aren't immune to "making stuff up" either. When stressed we often turn over the things partners and work colleagues say to us and construct an alternate reality, regardless of the facts, in which every new word or action just goes to reinforce either our self-doubt or the idea that the whole world is out to get us.

A friend recently told me about trying to get her sister who was in a mental health crisis, into a holiday home where she believed her sister would be happy. The sister negatively reframed this as "trying to make her live in a hut".

#112 Popularity manipulating.

This can happen in work teams or in families. These twats should be given a wooden spoon. Much like the nice-mummy competition, some people seem to need to win the 'I'm so much nicer than the other person' competition... and they will. They will go from person to person creating a narrative about each other person in the group in order to divide them. Don't engage with these situations. You'll always lose.

#113 Family comparisons.

Those who compare their kids, or their parents, with other people's, and find theirs wanting.

That's like comparing apples to oranges and finding oranges not to be appley enough. If you are in a family like this, all you can do is let it go. Apply the 'that's their problem' principle. To carry on the metaphor... if they don't like oranges as much as apples it's not your fault or your responsibility. Both fruits are equally delicious and nutritious.

Argumentative twats (and how to cope with them)

This next section is a bit of a therapy session for readers who can't help getting irrationally (or rationally) annoyed with the people/twats in your life. Because I'm old, I've lost a lot of arguments in my life. I know a bit about how to navigate arguments without resorting to name calling and anger. But If you do have trouble with people making you feel bad in an argument count to ten or twenty or thirty. You can use a mantra during those seconds to deflect the negativity. Mine is 'Healthy, Happy, Loving and Kind'. Then just smile and carry on the conversation in a different direction. You may need to smile and fib that you need to go to the toilet to take yourself away from the situation for a while. Your friend may think you have suddenly developed a weak bladder but that doesn't matter!

#114 "Your fault" blamers.

The difference between ' fault' and 'responsibility'. So, why is the difference between the word fault and responsibility important? After all, they're just words aren't they? Well, it goes back to how people react to these words, how they can, or can't make stuff up, on the back of an ill considered word.

Consider the difference when saying to a child "It's your fault you didn't do your homework" to "It's your responsibility to do your homework". The F word implies an intransigent situation, exasperation, even lack of love and respect. Whereas responsibility implies none of these negatives. Rather the belief in the person, that they're up to the job, that they can change the situation for themselves, that you respect them. In the mind of a child there is no loss of love and trust in the word responsibility. Rather the certainty that this situation (the situation where they failed to complete their homework) is an impermanent one, and you are certain your child is just about to regain control and doesn't need you giving them the double slap when they are already feeling a bit low about the situation.

Do we ever learn that exasperation with a teenager never works and can only have a negative effect on their self esteem? I don't think we do. And I don't think we learn it as adults dealing with each other either. This problem is not confined solely to the exasperation of parents towards their kids. It can also be just as damaging the other way around when kids grow up and their parents become elderly. Responsibility increases slowly as children grow and diminishes slowly as the aged fade. We need to understand how to encourage self-determination as soon as possible and not take it away, for as long as possible.

We also need to learn this patience with our partners and patiently hand them the keys that they can never find. This is because they never will, because it's not on their radar, because they have other skills and mental strengths. Of course I'm talking about myself here and my lovely husband who patiently puts up with all my failures of responsibility! Just maybe one day our loved ones will work out their own solution to the problem. Any discussion using the words fault and blame however, is likely to be continued into the courtroom.

#115 Defensive twattery.

This really must be just about all of us. If we could take the chips off everybody's shoulders we would all be much happier. We all need a good dose of no fault but responsibility training. We don't have to justify what's in the past, we just have to value what we are and get on with living now with one eye on the future.

Think about the people who aren't defensive. They are just getting on and doing things and making stuff and they are generally happy in their lives and in their conversations with others. They shrug off negativity and always have the right answers in a discussion. The defensive ones are always explaining themselves in terms of why their point of view is more justifiable and why yours isn't. It's been an epidemic on social media in the last few years. It seems like everyone is telling everyone else what they ought to be thinking based on their own defence of their life choices. Very few of us are immune to this. It's usually symptomatic of a certain degree of low self esteem or at least of not being exactly sure of your own place in the world.

There is a saying in Spain "no tiene abuela" which means "he hasn't got a grandma". It's usually used for people who brag or blow their own trumpet. It seems to me that they have something here. Grandmothers (and fathers) are for self-esteem. Their job is to love unconditionally. Parents tend to want the best for their children and often worry about whether the kids are taking all the opportunities and making the best of them etc. Grandparents are there just to love without any agenda. I didn't have a grandma and I think it shows.

I was definitely one of the defensive twats. I've just about given up defensiveness. Not completely. For example I had to cut a huge part of the intro to this book where I was trying to defend the subject in terms of "I'm really quite nice in spite of all these judgements". I realised the defence was not necessary. I'm getting there. It's really rather pointless to always be on the defensive. You never realise the real you. When I say realise, I mean of course in the sense of getting to where you want to be.

So how to stop being defensive? I can only say how I've dealt with it. First of all it's to understand that the only person whose world you are at the very centre of... is you.

And that nobody else is more interested in what you're doing or what you're thinking than you. So you can do and think whatever the hell you want, but just don't expect people to agree with you. And it's very much a waste of your valuable time trying to persuade someone else of your point of view if they aren't interested. They usually aren't. What's more they're allowed not to be. Secondly, once you've realised that you can't change anyone else's mind, that frees you not to bother trying. Getting the time and emotional energy back that you would have spent on that fruitless pursuit is very freeing!

Just be aware that there is a transition. The person who you used to have an uneasy and conflicted relationship with may not understand the new you and you may find yourself being dragged into your own old patterns of behaviour for a while. When you find that happening just stop. Count to ten and continue as the new you who doesn't have to try and win the argument. In fact there is no argument. Just your old way of being. Your defensive way.

Online it's much easier. You can just refuse to take the bait. There is a lady who I chat with online who is a bit of a conflictive person and who has many argument winning, bullying tricks. These days I am getting more able simply to refuse to answer the questions that get me into those downward cyclical discussions. Because defensiveness can get you right back into the grips of a negative and defensive thought process.

#116 Must win the argument!

Being on the defensive is only one of the two weak positions to get into in any discussion. The other is to be on the offensive. When that happens there are no winners because winners in an argument don't actually win anything. They don't get their opponents love, trust or any real concessions at all. Once the discussion escalates into an argument it is already lost on both sides. Usually both parties go away thinking less of each other, not more. If you can keep your head and recognise the trigger points for an argument and simply refuse to go there, you and your friend go away with a much more effective relationship the next time. But you have to handle it very carefully because it's still a manipulative action to walk away from an argument. You need to leave the other person time to cool down too. Nothing is gained by winning an argument. nor by 'flouncing'. However heated good natured discussions, where you might have different viewpoints, are useful and fun. The only ones you need to stop are where the good humour slips on either side.

It's also well worth remembering that there are two kinds of arguments. Those with people you care about (and thus care about what they think of you) and those who you need never come across again. With the first type you will need to offload. Also remember the other person has their own chips on their own shoulders and you really don't want to add to them. If you really feel you aren't in the wrong you definitely need to do some offloading of the stress which can be damaging to your health. Do some physical exercise. Go for a walk or a run or a swim. Maybe do some 'earthing' exercises. Put your hands on a solid wall and imagine the negativity flowing from your head through your hands and down into the earth. Really it doesn't matter what you think of this exercise or why it works. This sounds a bit 'new age' bullshitty, but I know from offloading negative energy after sessions as a helpline counsellor. It works. Then if you realise you were in the wrong you might have some apologising to do. Otherwise you're good to go. For real problem people there are block and mute buttons or their equivalent in real life. Either temporary or permanent time out... depending on whether you think their twattery is irredeemable, or not.

Twats in Packs

I don't join clubs because there's always one isn't there? Maybe a battle between two. One in a group is just a twat. Two are a liability and can destroy happy groups. Because I'm not very sociable, I've relied on a club-going friend for some of these.

#117 The 'emeritus' Neighbourhood Watch chair.

Chairpeople are so often the twattyest, rising to the top aren't they? This twat resigns, when he's sure nobody else wants the position; only to demand that he's reinstated with the word 'Emeritus' on the front of his title.

#118 The hobby club president.

I've heard stories about a few of these. But I was once actually in the middle of a group strop as the invited 'celebrity'. The chairperson decided to use the big event to resign dramatically and to give a vicious parting speech. At least, it sounded vicious. Fortunately I couldn't speak enough Swiss-French to know.

I've deliberately left most politicos out of this book, but they do also like to do the same spoiled-child 'flouncy' thing don't they?

#119 Volunteer ill treating twats.

Friend's twat choice - "People who attend events/clubs run by volunteers and have lots of ideas about what we're doing wrong... but don't want to volunteer their time in any capacity".

#120 People who take social crafting too seriously.

Friends twat choice - "Me and my friend got told off by some girls (from Harrogate) in a pottery class for not taking the class seriously enough. My friend replied - Ooh so, not a place to come and bond then?"

#121 Parents of kids in clubs.

Friend's twat choice: "when we were running a meeting on zoom - baking brownies - and despite both parents being in the kitchen they blamed us for a child's injury... at home!

The same parents also claimed mileage and bandages from the unit funds when the child had to go to the minor injuries unit for catching a toasted marshmallow and burning a hand!"

Parents can be awful in most children's clubs and classes. I taught English to a really great class of kids once and, unusually, all the parents were great too. If they had a problem with class days or times etc. I could refer them to one of the parents to co-ordinate. I never had to negotiate, just to teach.

Later I had a couple of groups where I didn't have the 'main parent hub'. There was so much conflict between the parents and even towards me about times of classes and whose little darling should be in which class. One pulled both their children out of their respective classes because I wanted to move her angel into a more appropriate class. I even had a divorcing couple, both of whom wanted their kids to continue in the class, but both told me to ask the other parent for payment! At that point I decided it was time to retire.

Driver twats

#122 Motorbikers and car drivers who take the silencer off their exhaust.

And the guy with a trailer in our village who never has anything in it, but never takes it off. The damn thing rattles over the loose cobbles in our plaza several times a day almost dislodging the teeth of any elderly local on the pavement.

#123 Car owners who won't turn the engine off while parked.

These twats stand in the street passing the time of day with their neighbours. One might imagine I'd get rationally annoyed with the time it takes them to have any thought for the person waiting to continue their day. Señora M tells Señor B about El Porro's bunions. I don't mind that so much. It's friendly, it's laid back, it's Spanish. What infuriates me is that they pretend they really are are just about to move and keep their dirty diesel engine running for five minutes. I'm terribly allergic to diesel fumes myself and I can't imagine it does much for little Jesus in the pushchair's lungs either.

#124 Indicate FFS!

What's that blinky thing? All Spanish drivers (almost literally). You know if they appear to be indicating that they did it once and don't know how to turn it off. Or they caught the indicator with their sleeve when reaching for a cigarette.

#125 Over large car for your needs?

If your car needs to look like a 'bully boy' you probably really need a van. The exception is if you have several young children and need safety and space. See also wealth-signalling twats and small dick energy (*ah sorry, that's the next book*).

#126 People who tailgate.

On motorways or any road - generally white BMW drivers and all Audi drivers in the UK. And EVERY driver in Spain.

#127 Car owners who don't appreciate 'small toy joy'.

(Revenge karma again) The petrol-head relative with an MG who couldn't be bothered to take a courtesy look at our new pride and joy (our first new car) saying "I've seen a Ford Escort before". He spent the next week trying to work out who, in his village, had put a note under the windscreen wiper of his (3rd vehicle) truck saying he should remove the disgraceful eyesore. Connecting the two events might have given him a giggle and saved a big headache. It was meant to be a gentle & humourous poke. I couldn't have known sweet little Devonshire villages really are full of uppity twats!

Selfish misbehaving twats

#128 Smokers.

Or rather a very large percentage of them including: people who smoke in the car while giving you a lift, after all it's their car and they are kind enough to give you a lift. Err no. Tell us if you're going to be that kind of twat in advance.

I've always had difficulty telling smokers not to smoke around me because I've always tried to be nice. I was a smoker, and I know how strong the addiction is. And so it's difficult to say this but addicts are the most selfish of all because they demand their right to foist their addiction on you. But here's why I can finally write what I think about this twattery and can finally not give a flying-one about whether the smoker likes me or not.

I was in the Doñana national park the other day with a bus load from my village. I always knew my friend's sister was a bit of a smoking twat. She insisted on lighting a cig in the middle of a heatwave in a very dry place while telling me that a few years ago the park suffered a devastating forest fire. Her husband is a firefighter FFS! There's no reasoning with these twats. The same one the other day, after I'd had a coughing fit from a backdraught from the fire, lit up within a couple of feet from me. This one smokes in her sister's house even though she's given up herself because of cancer she's still being treated for. The main thing that causes cancer is regular and repeated inflammation. But you're the problem for not allowing them their life choices; in this one's opinion.

When smokers talk about their 'right' to smoke I do understand their fight for their addiction, but they hold no rights over MY health. So now I don't care if I sound bossy and overbearing, shooing them out of my space.

Would I like a cigarette? No thanks. Not even to be more 'agreeable' to smokers.

Also smokers who reward your understanding of their need to smoke by leaving you with a stinky ashtray to clean out on your patio.

#129 Twats on buses.

People who won't stand for an older, clearly tired or struggling person or a young mum with kids on a bus. On the other hand the horrible woman who threw a strop at a young man with clear neurodivergence who was sitting in a disabled space. He said he had a bad foot and helpfully pointed to the other pram area at which point the woman threw a hissy-fit because she had 2 prams, instead of explaining. She then spent the rest of the very long journey looking daggers at the poor young man and bending another woman's ear about what a horrible specimen he was. I got off at the same stop as, and had a nice conversation with, the poor bent-eared woman who had also had her journey completely spoiled. Sometimes you just need to negotiate. I can content myself that bitter and twisted people age very badly. Karma.

#130 Car boot sale idiots.

Friend's twat choice: ask you how much something is... you say 10p, and they walk away. Apparently a Yorkshireman called after this twat "If tha' cant afford 10p tha' shunt be 'ere!"

#131 One star rating trolls.

They could be doing it out of envy or just a sad life. They 'out' themselves as 'reviewer trolls' by not giving a review to a hotel/Etsy store/book that usually has good reviews but by giving a malicious one star rating only, often with no explanation. Says more about the troll than it does about the book/goods/hotel.

So If you don't like being called a twat and want to give this book a low rating, fair enough, but do have the courage to review.

Make sure you don't out yourself as a twat in the review, though. Like the right winger who got my 'The Frugalist' book after I said on Twitter, "Right wingers don't like this book but they won't say why". He left a "Couldn't get past the rant at the beginning" review. What was it about a book with a clear anarchist sign on the front cover that suggested there wasn't going to be a (skippable) political commentary on the need to be frugal in the intro? Maybe turn the page (or flick on an ebook) and get past the intro.

I have noticed that left wing books (including mine) do get rating pile ons and it can even be a reverse recommendation. Where there are no reviews it's obvious that it's just political and where there are... it's even more obvious. Some of my favourite non-fiction books have some terrible ratings and reviews. Non-political books don't have these type of pile-on. Just the odd one-star troll.

#132 Plane seat kickers.

Come on parents! The odd wriggle and accidental kick is understandable, after all nobody can help if their kid has ADHD, but tolerance can only be stretched so far when it's your little twat, and not ours. If your kid really does have a medical condition please just apologise then we won't think you're a twatty parent.

#133 People who let off fireworks this century.

Leave private fireworks in the past where the biscuit tin of anticipation and eye damage danger belongs. Because there are always firework exhibitions and you can book them as part of major celebrations, there is now no need for private letting off of fireworks except sparklers and those little indoor birthday party things. So now it's either only misbehaving kids or arrogant, entitled adults who do it.

TV twattery

#134 Public figure/celeb twats.

Getting hold of the twat in yourself and realising that it makes you funny or entertaining is a skill. These people are nevertheless twats and provoke adoration or hatred. Even among this group there are two distinct types. Those who are hateable and those who are hateful. We shouldn't mix up the two. For example, off the top of my head I'd give you two hateable comedians that I rather like. Clarkson and Gervais. And then there are the not remotely funny celebs Hatie Kopkins and Wann Iddecome.

#135 Twats who were educated at media school 10-20 years ago editing shows.

Skipping about between stories especially on accidents and emergencies to fill time. "Back in Harrogate". Hang on. Weren't we there just 3 minutes ago? This style of program making is all over all the emergency programmes and the house-build programmes. It's not to build tension because all that is lost. It's simply annoying! It just looks like ridiculous time wasting in order to fill a particular time slot by use of repetition.

#136 Stupid section-breaks and timing announcements on "The Great" this or that.

Cooking, sewing, pottery etc. reality competitions. Dressing up, or pretending to do something related or ironically unrelated to the programme while spouting stupidly unfunny twatteries, must make some of these presenters die a little inside every time. They make my skin crawl.

I believe the art professionals have dug their heels in on this because it doesn't appear too much on art programmes. Too highbrow.

#137 Over 100% effort.

In interviews when being asked how much effort someone has put in or how much they want to win a competition. "I'm giving it 110 percent" is an understandable mild twattery. Much worse is doubling up or even more. 1000 percent effort or want does not exist. Program makers... stop making people up the idiot ante!

#138 Backstory stuffing.

Contestant's backstories: how sad can we make this one? How uplifting?

#139 Advertising twats.

When they pour blue water on sanitary towels. It's red guys! OK I'll let that pass. Some people are very sensitive and I see no reason to rattle your cages since the message is clear enough. The only thing I have issue with is the minimising of what a thoroughly bloody difficult and expensive thing to cope with periods are. I'm very glad that a few new ways of coping with them are now being invented, at least giving some choices in the matter of soaking up the bloody red stuff.

Ecology twats

#140 People who ignore or sneer at ancient wisdom because it's old.

For example one of these twats would sneer at the science at play in the old lady mopping the tiled floors in summer to keep her home cool. Her science. The cooling effect of evaporation. Too much like hard work this twat would say. These types would rather work for longer to pay the electricity for air conditioning, and then even more for the gym membership for a workout. They would rather look sweaty in public than mop a floor to keep cool at home.

#141 Companies who haven't put any effort into exploring other packaging choices.

And those who double wrap in plastic.

#142 People who don't put things in the right recycle bin when it's almost harder not to.

And people who leave rubbish around beauty spots even though there are plenty of bins to put the rubbish in. A few weeks ago I was at a 'mirador', a viewing point at a site of outstanding natural beauty. The place was littered with plastic bottles and crisp and chocolate packs and wraps. It IS possible that the wind had simply lifted some of the rubbish out of the bins, so I also have to give a twat point for the planner who decided that an open style of bin was the most appropriate for that area. And one to the rubbish collection services who clearly don't collect often enough.

#143 Fly tipping.

Clearly the tippers themselves are twats of the highest order but any political system that says it's OK to produce that much waste but which makes it more expensive to dispose of it correctly, is part of the problem.

#144 People who believe keeping all animals is bad for the planet.

I live in a rural area where goats are shepherded and milked. Black foot pigs, highly prized for the best Serrano ham, live relatively long, and it seems very happy, lives between the cork trees munching acorns. Both clean up the land between the trees thus making forest fires less likely and less devastating. Some of these people would rather have fields and fields of intensively grown soya with the ecological imbalance that creates. I'm definitely firmly in the 'eat less meat' camp. I'm flexitarian and my husband is vegetarian. But I do find radical veganism a bit challenging.

#145 Climate change denier twats.

The twat who had a go at Greta the climate activist. Challenging her that England had a 17 degree average that summer. Clearly not understanding all the meanings of the word 'average'.

Incidentally, more delicious karmic revenge for Greta haters - the guy whose car which had a "Fuck You Greta" notice in the window and was snapped being washed away in a flash flood. And of course Andrew Tate. I don't need to say any more.

#146 Twatty scientists.

Renewable energy deniers who believe the bull that they are fed. Here are some objections to solar I heard only 10 years ago from a Spanish geologist neighbour. Lovely lad... Twat! Of course he's changing his mind now as are we all but this is just to show how we can be conned by big energy propaganda when they don't want us doing something which might affect their bottom line.

"It takes up too much land".

Printable sheets to attach to roof areas; ceramic tiles as collectors for patio areas; carports in every supermarket car park; and what about the acres of rail tracks which could easily power the trains! The underused spaces are already there. No need to add much to that. But if you want to, there are lots of fruit growers in areas with a lot of sun that need a certain amount of shade. Part-covering greenhouses with photovoltaics could provide that shade and power the growers and their neighbourhood. This would also reduce water use. What about airsource, ground source and water source heat collectors? All are forms of solar heating power. Research into newer storage of power, for example salt batteries in basements etc., is still ongoing. The more that is invested in these alternatives the more viable they will become. That's why 'big energy' don't want them.

"It's too expensive."

Since I had this conversation the price has more than halved. You can now pay back your investment in 3 years instead of 7. The more investment in a technology, the more efficient and popular it becomes. Then the cheaper it can be. Think how expensive the gigabytes/terabytes in your hand held computer tablet were just a decade ago.

"The sun doesn't produce enough power. Nuclear power is more efficient."

Really?! Are you trying to tell me that that huge hot nuclear reactor isn't enough to power this little planet? Actually everything we are currently using in the form of fossil fuels is just stored power from the sun in one form or another. We'd just be taking it in a more direct form.

"It's unreliable."

There is a point there, but then storage and use of gas, coal oil, hydroelectric, wind etc. can fill the gap. Just because it isn't 'on' all the time doesn't make it not potentially the biggest and best source of power... at least in countries like sunny and windy Spain. Storage technology is improving. But technology only improves with investment. You don't find solutions if you aren't looking for them.

Pompous and supercilious twats

#147 Medal wearing especially by royals.

It seems needy doesn't it?

#148 'Our servicemen' sycophancy.

I know this could be unpopular with families of servicemen but let me explain. To my mind it's weird and creepy when it's over-the-top flag waving for those who have been shipped off to needless wars. Necessary defence is a different matter and the line, admittedly, is difficult to draw. Even worse when those with PTSD are left mentally broken and homeless but those who use it to create jingoism and xenophobia, don't give a damn for those real people's lives.

Obviously there is also a need for powerless parents and partners of soldiers both serving and fallen, to feel that their sons/daughters/partners have not died for nothing and that their death is valued... that grief is real and understandable, so I'll leave it there.

#149 People who think the only source of all truth and all wisdom is Google.

Google ranks what the public asks for a lot, and those who have paid a lot for SEO experts to rank them. You can pick and choose your 'truth' from the very many truths out there.

#150 People who disagree with everyone else's life choices.

These are the twats who want you to join them in their misery and so they criticise your life choices.

We are, or should be, all responsible for our own life choices. Of course those choices can come with hidden strings, especially if you choose to be with a person or people who have their own life goals which may differ from yours. That can complicate the matter.

They also tend to be the same people who criticise immigrants for wanting to choose to live in 'their' place. It sounds like hatred, but I think it may be a cover for a repressed envy.

#151 Fact checker twats.

Checking your facts is important. But blindly believing your first search on Google is barely better than no checks at all. Fact checkers have now been proved to be buyable. Some fact checking sites have been set up for political ends. Don't trust the trust-seller! If you are a fact checker twat (one who screeches "that's not true" and cites a fact checking site) take a second to change your words to "may not be true".

#152 "I never ask a question unless I know the answer" twats.

This twat was provided by a friend who knows someone who actually said this! These people want to trip you up, but never want to be caught not knowing something themselves. They are usually the most emotionally ignorant and needy of all. This twat is related to the one who insists on telling you what their IQ score is. I've never met one of these who wasn't desperately short of love.

Bad twattitudes

#153 People with more than one 'face'.

People who appear friendly but have one public face and another actual opinion.

For example a special behaviour for social situations which is not how they are in one-to-one contexts. So difficult for neurodivergent people on any part of the spectrum to read. It leads to so much confusion and pain. Often called 'treading on eggshells' some of these people/situations are on the twats list below. Of course the other side of the coin is that those people who expect a certain form of conforming behaviour are equally confused by those who just don't 'get it'.

#154 Those who suck all the air out of a room.

Drama queens who address every social situation in terms of how it affects them. Girl/boy sometimes it has nothing to do with you. Maybe that's what you don't like?

#155 Everyone's a critic.

Those who openly and publicly criticise each other in social situations (as opposed to gentle teasing round a friendly dining table).

#156 Going Dutch.

Those who when going for a meal and 'going Dutch' do not understand the need for the poorer members of the group to ask for tap water rather than the expensive bottled stuff.

#157 Credit stealers.

Those who take all the credit for an event that they actually undermined... once it is obvious it has been successful.

#158 Not competitive!

Those who regularly state I'm not competitive". Oh you really are! This one enters competitions regularly and usually wins.

#159 You're my favourite!

People who play the "you're my favourite but s/he is so difficult!" game with each member of a group.

#160 "I've got more problems than you" twattery.

Where the person who bleats the loudest about their problems gets everyone else to take notice. While the quiet ones get their needs ignored. What we are all looking for with our 'I've got more problems than you' approach, or conversely our hiding of our problems lest we are judged for them, will not be cured by more sympathy, but by caring less about people's unnecessary judgement of us.

#161 Those who call positive personal attributes deficiencies.

Reported insult-twattery from a friend. Someone called her "untrammelled" in a scathing letter. It was intended to be hurtful, of course. Being untrammelled seems to me a delightful alternative to being constantly trampled upon by others' expectations. It turns out that the person who called her out just delights in using big words he doesn't necessarily understand. I've read his book and I've never seen as many inappropriately used homophones.

Note: rein, reign, rain. It's free rein people! As in the horse's rein is loose... so he can go where he wants.

I get irrationally annoyed when pompous people validate themselves by using big words, and then use words and expressions incorrectly... and then blame spell-checker. Twats!

Religious twats

#162 Godbotherers in general.

Personally I see religion as a type of compulsive behaviour. A sort of insurance against fear. Some are mildly deluded, some are seriously dangerous. I can live side-by-side with them if they only use their religion for the good of their own mental health and occasionally for the good of mankind. I appreciate that local culture and cohesiveness can be improved by shared belief and by regular rituals and practises that bring them together. However it more often than not strays into the bad areas that follow. Then there are the American style religious 'influencers'. I can't help saying, atheistically of course, *"oh my good god!"* Do they really fall for that line?

#163 Cardinal kiddyfiddlers.

You got into religion because you were scared of your own weirdness. Yes you are odd and creepy, and now you're using your position of power and the awe you inspire to abuse. No ifs nor buts. Get a grip. Just because you find someone attractive doesn't mean you have to act on it. Get yourself some therapy. Leave the kids alone. Oh and by the way your religion is bollocks and you know it. Your idea of religion I definitely don't have to respect!

#164 Christian/religious emotional abuse of children.

It's all about guilt and forgiveness and putting the power of forgiveness into the hands of a few more powerful and greedy people. Giving someone religion as a child is like implanting a control chip. Hypnotising someone with a trigger word that at some point in the future can be used to control them. It can take a lifetime to get over the notions implanted into you as a child by even well meaning adults.

Even as a four or five year old I had notions of death as something I should fear not having any power over.

My mother taught us a prayer "Now I lay me down to sleep, I pray the lord my soul to keep... And if I die before I wake I pray the lord my soul to take." Sounds pretty innocuous maybe, but when you get to school and the ideas of heaven and hell come in that's where the fear can start to be triggered and next come the 'better than or worse than' messages. The only person who should have the power to make you feel guilty or to forgive you... is you. Instead of teaching religious studies try teaching empathy studies and you can put religious beliefs right back where they belong: in history and psychology classes.

#165 Hellfire twats.

Some say they are religious because of the afterlife, but I've found, from limited experience admittedly, that most people who are religious fear death more than those who don't. I have a simple idea of 'afterlife'. Everyone in your life who you touched in any way goes on to build their life with a tiny bit of your energy in it. The 'rest' of you, atoms and energy, is assimilated into the earth, water and air around you to make up a tiny part of millions of sentient and non sentient beings.

#166 People who object to teaching inclusivity in schools.

The irony of religious parent groups carrying "stop brainwashing our children" placards. Parents who get totally rabid and talk about teaching "the practice of" homosexuality in schools. Stop overstating it. You are undermining your argument by using that one extra word 'practice' where it is not warranted or truthful. They are not teaching 'the practice'. Introducing sexual 'practice' to very young children is not what it's about. As part of family relationship education they are teaching the 'fact' of homosexuality and as part of inclusivity they are teaching that it's OK to be different. Just as the fact of religious faith should be taught in schools but not the faith itself IMO.

My children went to a C of E school and learned about Diwali and Ramadan which is as it should be. They came home to their atheist mother and asked questions about religion and I would say "some people believe this or that" When they asked me about my beliefs I answered them truthfully that I didn't hold these beliefs but I was prepared that if they grew up to take a religion I would still be their loving mother and still would support them. I taught my kids that lying, cheating and bullying were wrong and I was pretty firm on that one. I'm prepared to admit, that doesn't necessarily prepare them to 'get ahead' in current society but that was the chance I had to take.

To say "stop brainwashing our children" is to ignore the irony that teaching a religion is a form of brainwashing. Give your children open minds; it's the greatest gift you can give.

When children are old enough to ask questions they are old enough to be given the answers but of course maturity varies from child to child and the answers vary from parent to parent and it seems there is no universal truth when it comes to sex, sexuality nor religion.

#167 People who call perversion on adult consensual activities.

The sexually confused and fundamental religious homophobes. The problem with most people who get hung up on either side of religious and sexual arguments is that often they have their own axe to grind and that own axe in the case of the religious nut is the fear that some of their own inappropriate thoughts are evil and so must be stamped out by imagining that they are the temptation of the devil and not just some passing thought.

This brings me neatly on to sexual perversion. Some people would want to take my 'we love who we love' statement from the sublime to the ridiculous by saying in that case it's OK to love children or conflating the love of another human being of the same gender with being someone who wants to have sex with animals.

I believe that every human occasionally or often has inappropriate thoughts: from the light passing thought, to the downright weird. We are almost all able to pass over them and recognise them as inappropriate and throw them straight out. For example I don't think I'm any weirder than anyone else when I have dreams about sexual liaisons with other people even though I'm married. In fact the funniest things sometimes happen. Here I am in a totally safe space (the dream) able to do what I want and yes I have had a very exciting dream life… telling my latest 'fling' "Sorry but I'm happily married". Dammit! I can tell my husband about this because he's secure but I might not tell him about every single dream. Nor would I want to know about his. Suffice it to say some of my dream behaviour wouldn't be appropriate in real life!

So now what I truly believe is that the out and out ranting homophobe is afraid of his inner thoughts and perhaps his dream life and worries that these are manifestations of 'the devil trying to tempt him'. The way he tries to cope with them is to try to exorcise the whole idea. What a shame. Dream life can be fun! I still smoke in my dreams for example. And I still fancy a cig from time to time. An inappropriate thought. As long as I don't smoke in real life it's all fine. It's the same with inappropriate sexual thoughts. The more fearful we are of them perhaps the more hung up we get on them? That could be a better way of looking at the problem than simply deciding that the homophobe must by definition be homosexual. The more you worry about a thought and the more you try to push it out of your mind, the more it pushes its way back in. So my thought for the radical homophobe or the weird self flagellating types is:

Let those thoughts pass by uninterrupted and they'll soon be out of your system. Unless of course you really are more attracted to members of your same gender in which case no problem. If you are certain that you aren't, you can now move on and do something more useful with your life once you've examined this thought and let it pass.

#168 Conservative religious lawmaker twats.

Those who don't believe in bodily autonomy.

The older I grow the more I see the whole notion of God as mediaeval. All religions are controlling and ultimately 'radicalising'.

#169 The religious right wing in general.

They don't realise that Jesus was a socialist and are terrified of the word because they have been taught to equate socialism (seeing your fellow man as equal to you) with evil!

For example espousing 'family values' and at the same time being homophobic, while spending time in hotel rooms with underage boys. Also 'pro-lifers' who are very interested in the contents of a woman's womb, no matter how young or endangered the mother or the clump of cells, but very uninterested when it becomes a child that needs housing, feeding and clothing or indeed the life of any child in a war torn country if that child happens to come from one of their non-favoured ethnic groups.

Propagandist twats

#170 Twats causing culture wars and pack mentality episodes.

People are rounding on and organising vitriol on politicians and celebrities for making comments which we deem offensive this year even though we didn't in the year the comment was made. We don't allow U turns when realisation dawns that a policy, a speech or an incident was wrong. We do applaud people sticking to their guns in the face of mounting evidence that they are wrong though. This is totally back to front.

#171 Twats who use "Woke, do-gooder and leftie" as insults.

I have ceased to care whether people like or agree with me or not, because time for making a change to the world is running out and we are in danger of leaving the world a poorer and less fair place than it was when we 'inherited' it as lucky and rather spoiled post war 'baby boomers'. We had a world where people recognised the folly of war and inequality and took steps to ensure that everyone had access to a national health service and social security.

I've recently seen the moneyed classes attempting and succeeding to dismantle this for their own benefit.

Whenever a group achieves the power it seeks they become less open to outside opinions. At the far end of that process they end up screaming vitriol at people who question their group and its activities employing the very behaviours that they accuse their opponents of. It can happen that the bullied become the bullies. This can lead to a wave of anti-whatever opposition against the whole of the identity that has spawned its little coagulated radical hate-group core. This has happened with the whole transgender issue which has been radicalised on both sides now. You're either in... or out. On one side or the other. I'm an outsider to all these groups. But a world where feeling free not to fit in is as acceptable as any self identification as part of any group or subgroup. Yes I think I may actually be happiest in the subgroup numbering one.

On the other hand there are beautiful stories of people waking up. I have watched a very lovely lady I have known for a lot of years moving from white middle class privileged Tory voting tribe, to a free spirited intellectual creative. She clearly never fit perfectly into the former identity. She once told me off for swearing on social media. Now she's as sweary and leftie as the rest of us.

#172 Twats who envy... at the same time as criticising other people's life choices.

There are people who suggest that creatives should knuckle down to a 'proper job'. They suggest their own life path as the obvious best alternative. To them my question is:

When is a good time to start doing what you do best?

Did those who became well known artists, musicians, actors or even inventors think more about how they were going to make a living than how they were going to solve the problems that would help them create the next 'thing'? No.

Ignore the twats who don't call creativity a 'proper job'. They have made their own decisions and should leave you to make yours.

I am an artist and a writer. Apparently, because I'm not rich, I've been wasting my time. Who told me this? Well just about every one of my wealthier friends and relatives from whom I needed help during a life threatening illness. Did this make me feel contrite? No, actually it made me angry. Not just for myself but for all creative people who haven't yet developed the strength to know and ask for their worth.

The fact that creative people tend to be more humble about their worth and money shufflers are overvalued, is actually pretty bad for the growth of a mentally healthy and culturally interesting society, however that is the way we have gone for centuries!

Greed is *not* good. It is temporarily successful. What it doesn't do is give everyone the most contented life they could live. What happens however is that those who haven't achieved happiness in wealth, envy and stamp on those who have achieved happiness in spite of a lack of wealth. The amount of support the underpaid occasionally need is nowhere near the real worth of the wealth they have forgone, and the smallness of their footprint on this earth.

Sales twats

Remember all salesmen are potential twats

Why do we buy 'stuff' that is advertised to us? It has as much to do with addiction to being enough as it does to wanting to have enough and it has nothing at all to do with our needs.

You really don't have to sell anything we really need, you just have to put it visible enough in the marketplace. That is marketing. But salesmen are pushing things you don't need which they make you feel will enhance your life, or even that your life is less complete or that you are less successful without it. Don't buy it! Take charge of your own decision making on what and how much you need. Don't buy the notion that you have to have everything that is shiny and put in front of you. Don't lose the wonder and pleasure in the things you have.

#173 The twat who trains other people to earn lots of money (more than their share).

This one pulls his degree and masters to show that he's well qualified to pronounce that there isn't enough money for pensions. Quite likeable, if misguided, this one. He has a bit of a hang up about making enough money to live comfortably and claims to have 11 properties. So that makes him qualified to talk about pensions and how they can't be afforded. He has suffered (relative) poverty and it made him feel suicidal. He managed to drag himself back to wealth but still thinks that's possible for everyone. And doesn't see that the cause of some people not having enough... is other people having too much.

#174 Youtube salesmen walking towards the camera.

Especially those in Spain. Especially the smug silver fox. What a twat!

#175 Offers on memberships that make you go through several steps before you even see the price.

If that works, then the public must be dimmer than I thought. And it does, so, clearly they are. What I find refreshing are sales that stay away from all that funnelling crap and just tell you what they give you and what it will cost.

Contributed by Geraldine (RIP) of Whatpissesmeoff.

#176 Kickbacks.

Big companies who want kickbacks for example for stocking certain generic drugs. This can only increase the price and holds the suppliers to a type of protection racket. "You don't pay the kickback, we don't stock your product."

#177 Call centre person to person advertising calls.

In order to refuse as politely as possible, we always say - "This is a sales call isn't it?" "No, they counter, it's information." "Are you hoping to sell me a product or service?" is our next question. If they defend by using the information line again or begin to stammer we just say, "Thanks very much but you're wasting your time". Look we know you have to earn a living but if you can't take no for an answer OR if your 'job' involves taking someone for a ride you got this coming:

On a bad day when you're feeling impatient simply say "Oh excuse me a moment I have some paint I need to watch drying". And put the handset face down on a pillow or next to a speaker blaring out some of your least fave tunes.

On a good day when you have time you can start a game. See how good an actor you are. Play the gullible target. When they say your Windows computer seems to have some issues or your bank account details aren't safe you can play along but *never* give any real details at all. Have a list of fake answers. Fake ID and passwords, fake first pets name, fake maiden name or if you're a gold star wind-up merchant a fake line of code you can pretend to read off your machine. Practise typing 'the quick brown fox' or just tapping any key over and over again but remember to press the spacebar occasionally otherwise it doesn't sound right. Not that that matters. See if you can pass yourself off as someone with a brain disease or a child of 10. The world of acting practice is open to you and you'll be craving a con attempt before long!

Scamming and conning twats

#178 Mobility aid scam twats.

Their target demographic is the pensioner with mobility issues. These people are *very* plausible. Be ready for them and make sure your elderly parents are ready for them. My mother-in-law must be on their target list after once being talked into buying a very expensive Craftmatic bed. I say they're very plausible because I've seen one off since who was trying to sell her a chair and had another relative see one off. Both of us report that we weren't sure until after they were gone whether we were actually being rude to a very nice person. They get themselves into your/your elderly relative's house by pretending to be from some mobility or comfortable living organisation and suggesting you may be eligible for a new 'thing' to make your difficult life more bearable. They make you believe they are attached in some way to the local authority or the health service and they are simply coming to assess your needs. They are very capable in the art of acting offended or affronted if you suggest that they may be trying to scam you and also very sympathetic and helpful if you suggest you can't afford their overpriced bed. They talk of finding ways to help you. They suggest your family could and should help you. They don't leave for hours and then only when you've signed their paper to make them just go away.

First of all don't let *anyone* in on the basis of a phone call from them to you. Ask for their name and their department and write it down. Call the council the next day (definitely not on a number that *they* give you, but on a number you obtain privately from the internet or from a letter heading from your local council). Ask if this person actually exists and if so if you can be put through to them.

If they are already in your house and you're alone, call a relative or friend and ask them to come round. You can say it's to help you decide. If you have had problems with scammers before, arrange a safe word or phrase. For example you could say "I'm having difficulty making any decisions" to let your relative know that this appears to be a scam. When that person has arrived use the words No and Go very firmly and suggest you will call the police if they don't leave. Be prepared to carry out your threat.

#179 The gas con twat.

Especially prevalent in areas with butane/propane bottles only. They pretend they are from a government safety scheme. Just don't let them in. Yes, we got caught out. But they got 'done' when we reported them.

#180 Internet scamming twats.

I love having fun with these people. The fake Facebook friend for example. "Have you heard the good news? You can claim free money." That one. First of all ask them a ridiculous question like "are you still making those cats?" and when they say "Yes Lol" "And the monkeys?" Then usually follows a conversation where they try desperately to insert their script into my fake incredulousness or my ignoring of their side of the conversation completely.

The "your computer isn't working" twat who starts off with an obvious lie about his name. This neither appeals to the racist (who won't talk to furriners). Nor to the anti racist, who recognises the con and in between it just sounds pathetic.

#181 The 25 page book twats.

This one is personal! They self publish very poor quality books based on someone else's work. They are all over Amazon cluttering up the place and confusing and duping book buyers. You can often see them from the fact that English isn't their first language. Their author names are weird, backwards, in capitals. They have about 4 pages of craft publications and quizzes on TV shows. They have taken all this work from blogs and other people's books. Look for "look inside" and if it isn't there look for the back cover. Usually it's empty.

#182 Book publishing-con twats.

We just love your book! It saddens me to see so many would-be self-published authors falling for the ego-boost of being 'accepted' by a publisher that will ultimately relieve them of 4 or 5 thousand for publishing and receiving a couple of boxes of books. Similar to the model agencies that used to tell young naive women they were beautiful and then charge a fortune for taking their photographs. Why do people fall for it?

Education twattery

#183 Twats who want to make education boring and inaccessible.

Why don't teachers themselves stand up against the ordering of education into graphs and charts showing improvements in all areas, or none at all? This does nothing for neurodivergent children except calculate their worst possible score in their least favourite subjects and makes them failures at everything. Since all kids are somewhere on a spectrum it seems we're educating for banality. I have a feeling that those who have had a banal education themselves want to be sure nobody else can out-think them and that is why they keep intelligence and creative thinking at a very slow simmer.

#184 Teaching languages through grammar.

This is the way foreign language is routinely taught in schools, especially in Spain. Why? It's boring and obscure and a big turn off for at least 50% of the students who would be likely to be any good at it. When I look at grammar tables it looks more like maths to me than the joy and art that is language. Odio odias odiat. I taught English for a while to young Spanish kids. Because I didn't know how one should teach I taught through play and especially word games. The kids I taught, learned, because they wanted to learn.

#185 Teaching maths without physical and visual aids.

Thank goodness this is dying out!

#186 "Rounded education" twattery.

So when we try to smooth out the achievements of children at school forcing science down the throat of an arts student to make them more rounded and consistent educationally, we are really knocking off the peaks of their potential.

Misogynist, misandrist, narcissistic and psychopathic twats

"The enemy isn't men, or women, it's bloody stupid people and no one has the right to be stupid." Sir Terry Pratchett.

#187 Ignorant misogynist jokers.

Men who make jokes about leaving the toilet seat up but don't want to hear the medical reasons why they shouldn't.

Ooh this is one of my favourite rants. These twats love to tell toilet seat up toilet seat down jokes which in their minds are merely humorous observations on the difference between men and women. It is the perfect lowest common denominator area for humour, and for the idiots who spout it indiscriminately. So, for you Mr toilet seat twat and for all other young men in need of a little education: either raise the toilet seat before you use the toilet and then put it down after or be prepared to hear and understand the medical reasons why women want you to do so.

"Ugh" you'll say, "too much information", you'll say. "This conversation just got weird" you'll typically say. Well remember we didn't want to have to tell you we just wanted you to put the toilet seat down without asking questions.

This is one of the cases where you really should have listened when we said "because I said so" when you were young. But since you don't seem able not to grow up with the idea that you can question and make fun of this request, OK. You asked for it!

Women who have several babies or even one big baby do get badly damaged by this. They don't constantly push this indignity under your nose and whinge about it but they do have to suffer certain health problems such as rectocele, cystocele and prolapsed uterus. Look them up if you don't understand what these are before you make a fool of yourself and have to suffer the indignity of a strong woman embarrassing you with information you don't want to hear in front of your friends.

Let me make all this easy for you. All these medical complications of childbirth are pretty damn common among middle aged and older women (because we gave birth to you smug bastards). This means that certain parts of their anatomy are more likely to come into contact either with the toilet seat itself or with the hand they had to use to put the toilet seat back down which you left up. And generally there are no sinks inside toilet cubicles to then wash their hands before sometimes touching sensitive and easily infected areas.

Then the women in your lives may catch urinary tract infections. Some of these may even find their way back to you! Some of them after several repeat infections may get severe cystitis or even bladder cancer. Because all your 'bits' are always on the outside and have very protective layers, you can pretty much put the toilet seat up and down with impunity knowing your hand will never touch the softer more easily infected interior parts of your anatomy.

So, put the f***ing toilet seat down. We didn't want to have to tell you why... but it's not funny!

#188 Misogyny enabling twats.

My neighbour bless her, very sweet old lady but she did make the mistake of telling me I ought to be washing down my shutters. Thus ensuring I *never, ever* get caught doing so, and my husband has a new job. But not this week. If she finds my slightly dusty blinds offensive she can wash them herself, if she likes. The very next week another neighbour started demolition and rebuilding next to her house. Dust everywhere... karma.

While I'm on that one, twats in social situations on the subject of washing up. Don't drag me back into your gender stereotypical housewifery. If you want to wash up in the middle of a party, please feel free. I don't but will happily do my share at MY leisure. It's taken me a lifetime to get half way out of that one. If you've ever had a partner that keeps you in the manor (lady of the) style, maybe you owe them that. I haven't; and I don't owe anyone subservience.

#189 FGM ignorers.

Women's problem... not important, he says.

I have had an argument that got very heated indeed with one of my nearest and dearest who said there were more important things to worry about. I imagine if they went around removing fifty-something men's penis tips so that they could not enjoy sex, it might just change his mind about the importance of this matter. In case he's reading this... your evaluation of the importance of this issue... is still stupid.

#190 Belittling behaviour twats.

We see you, we really do.

Those of us who have ever lived with a controlling partner never get over the experience. There are two types of us. Those who expect it and go straight back into it. And those who recognise it and avoid it like the plague that it is.

These twats are often described as 'charming'. I wonder if Prince Charming, married Cinderella, having looked for a biddable girl to clean his own house and cut her off from her father and family and was a womaniser for the rest of his life.

My revenge-karma for a controlling twat. A song contest win for a song about the ex, who told his wife (me) her songwriting was too self indulgent and would never be any good. The song was a blues about that relationship. The last words in the winning song were, incidentally, "revenge is sweet".

Unfortunately controlling behaviour taints children of controlling parents/carers to some extent even if they despised that behaviour in their own parent/s.

#191 The 'alpha male'.

They are always a bit beta IMO. There are a few around. They are just sad scared misogynists with a simian habit of jutting their bottom jaw out just slightly when talking to someone (usually a woman) that they want to think is beneath them. These aggressive micro expressions aren't that hard to pick up guys. You make yourselves look silly and underdeveloped emotionally. Ever felt like telling a Millennial British Male that they are seriously wasting their carefully honed misogynistic disrespect on you? Yeah me too. But it'd be a waste of MY time.

#192 People who judge everyone's capabilities by the same standards.

This is too easy to get right so nobody should be making this mistake. These people have no time for the poor, the sick, the lonely (fill in difficulty) because they say, they managed to pull themselves out of poverty/sickness/loneliness. They are likely to make a big deal about lazy benefit claimants for example but worship lazy billionaires. They call the welfare state "The Culture of Dependency" and say we have to get rid of it. Personally I'd like to get rid of rich bastards being dependent on the hard work of poor people for insulting wages so they can profit massively and sit on their asses judging others as 'lesser'. But there you go. Universal Basic Income has been proven to work.

Not everyone is provided with the same capabilities, and resilience is difficult to acquire if you have never been taught it. So, hating those who started where you started and stayed there, is definitely on my top of the twats list.

#193 People who tell *you* how *you* think and how *you* have come to your decisions.

I've been told I must have got them from the papers, from online chatter and outrage, or even more misogynistically... from my husband! Is this a modern post division politics behaviour? The same people who tell you very firmly that you are disrespecting their intellectual prowess. Weird & semi-narcissistic perhaps? Certainly projection.

#194 Narcissistic controlling twats.

This is way too big a twattegory for me to deal with effectively here. And anyway there are experts in the subject who are far more worth listening to. I like to think there may be grades of narcissism though. Maybe that's because some of the people I know with minor forms of these traits, I don't want to consider or label as narcissists. Just a little fond of telling other people who and what they are. There are people who like to control the narrative by small acts of omission or small additions to the truth. When a narcissist can't control you they move to controlling how other people see you. It's hard to stay above it, but you really have to. If you engage, your protestations are often ineffective against the perceived genuineness of the controller.

Eventually people may see these control techniques. Sadly it sometimes takes years and hurts relationships which can be painful short term.

If you have a slightly controlling person on the peripheries of your life there's one thing you might notice: they sling insults at you fairly regularly especially when they are failing to control you. The insults may reach their mark and you may spend hours, days or even years wondering whether you really are the person that they accuse you of being. Often those accusations are indirect, to third parties and very difficult to work out. However one truth seems to me to be evident about these insults. They are almost always a form of projection. Once you recognise that, the barbs can't stick.

Don't bother calling a narcissist out though. You will always appear to be in the wrong. But when you know, as long as you don't engage and as long as you keep that person at arm's length, you are safer. My hope and to a certain extent my experience has been, if you stay true to yourself that eventually the world will see what is happening and your relationship with the other manipulated people can be even stronger because they can see how trustworthy and stoical you are.

I've mentioned gaslighting before. If you suspect or have a controlling relative or co-worker, check that out and also look up DARVO techniques. If you are a woman, and choose to stay with a narcissist because of financial reasons, you need to get some strength from somewhere sooner rather than later. This won't get better. There will be helping organisations in your area. If you can't find them, ask the Samaritans or the police. I know women who have stayed with controlling partners all their lives. Sadly it seems to get worse with their old age and infirmity.

Identity twats

#195 "You must choose sides" twats.

One thing that I believe contributes to a friend of mine's frustration when getting into discussions with me (no, let's not call them discussions, they are full-on arguments) is the fact that I refuse just to identify with any fixed point of view. My friend is and was by profession a powerful debater and she uses her intellect very cleverly, but like a weapon. It may be that because I spent a large part of my life simply watching those weapons being wielded and refusing to engage with them that I'm not just not the normal soft target. I'm not any kind of target. I simply refuse to draw the target at all.

This must be intensely frustrating for someone who is educated in adversarial work and trained and successful at winning. Identifying a target and the weakness of the target's argument. Aim your very best weapon and fire. It must absolutely infuriate her that I refuse to have a sticking post to nail my colours to. I refuse to have a single identity that I don't waver from. I guess that makes any idea of a target to argue with or indeed at, a frustrating mirage. My friend, who likes a good argument and loves coming out on top, ends up angered and befuddled that she doesn't know what I stand for. The fact is... there is rarely any single fact to be had on any subject. I like to be able to change my mind and so it is difficult for others to say I'm wrong. I'm as likely to admit I was wrong yesterday as not. I think I'm difficult to target from the point of view of an 'I'm OK you're not OK' targeter.

Unfortunately the whole idea of 'identifying as' is riven with problems. Damned if you do, damned if you don't. On an individual physical level you crave the safety of a tribe and all the power and force for change that tribe has. You have to compromise the idea of individual identity in order to feel safe and powerful. Those who don't want to join any forceful group at all will always be the outsiders. The weird ones. But are the weird ones a tribe in themselves?

I always had a joke about myself that I was an anti-ism-ist. It was my way of identifying myself as a weird one who absolutely refused to join any group who would have me. I used to say things like "I have my Annual General Meeting in a phone box" and "if you want to join the movement I'll have to leave". I wasn't sure what I meant by that but it was all about refusing to be labelled. I was what used to be called 'contrary'. I was both comfortable and uncomfortable with that. Comfortable because I knew there was never any chance I could be any different and uncomfortable because I suffered from the constant self enquiry and bombardment of a sort of existential doubt, and the constant admission of the probability that 'I might be wrong'.

#196 TERFs.

This is a long one. You can skip it if you don't have an issue with transgender people.

I didn't even know what a TERF was when I started writing this book. Then I met one. I have never seen so much hatred in a person. But I recognised it as fear. Terrible crippling fear of men.

I can absolutely understand there being a question of whether people with a genetic physical strength advantage should compete in sport on the same level. On the other hand. I don't really understand or care much for sport. If I did, I might suggest a special category. Surely it would make more sense to separate sporting opponents by various classes, such as weight classes in boxing, than by gender.

Terfy-ness seems to me as bad as racism. They imagine because someone has once made aggressive comments online that the behaviour of this one person (whoever they are) represents transgender people as a whole. For otherwise intelligent people this is the oddest of odd beliefs. I can only think that these people are seriously damaged and afraid. But we don't allow the fact that someone was once attacked by a person of colour to suggest that all that race of people are attackers. Oh actually we do. That has to stop too.

My 'friend' is transphobic and more than a bit bullying in her conversational style. Because of this I find her really difficult to converse with. Admittedly she has had very deep and genuinely held hang ups about gender and the power of men. Apparently (I didn't know until she told me) there is even a word for feminists who struggle with the idea of men being uncomfortable with their gender. Gosh haven't we all struggled with this one though. I have. Especially when a story hit the media, over a decade ago, about a man who was having a baby. It was clear to me at that time that this man had a womb at that point and was therefore born female. I didn't realise the person I was having this conversation with at the time was also struggling with their gender identity. But I no longer struggle with this because that was one single event showing the greyest of grey areas.

I'm lucky enough to have a very eloquent relative who is now married to a transgender man and also because one of the early apparently male loves of my life later became a woman. Incidentally, one of the things I liked about him was his gentleness which I could now redefine as femininity. The fact I couldn't cope with him wanting to wear my underwear simply meant I wasn't the right partner for him or I should say her... is all.

I am told, by my friend, that transgender women are stealing the word woman and have no right to do so. So how would my friend deal with her fear of men? Which is, incidentally, a fear of men... not of women but actually seems to be all about the possession of a penis. Well, for a start, she would ban all people with penises from using the ladies toilets. Let's not call them rest rooms shall we, because I don't know many people who actually rest there and if we need rest and a sit down surely a better solution would be to provide rooms for people to rest in such as waiting rooms in train and bus stations perhaps?

Identifying transgender women who still have their original plumbing would be a little difficult. Not so much in the United States where the toilet stalls seem to be high enough for one to identify if the occupant is standing up or sitting down to relieve themselves, possibly leading to some very weird behaviours on behalf of the 'gender police' and the very odd idea that I would be identified as transgender since I stand up to wee. Being in possession of a lifesaving ileostomy means I have a little bag with a tap and why would I bother sitting down? Conversely one of my nearest and dearest prefers to sit down to wee, being very tall and not wanting to splash himself with the backflow from the sheer force of his stream.

I put this point to my friend. My friend, incidentally, self identifies as left wing when she has lived so long in the London area as to have become neoliberal to the point of being right wing (that self identification thing)... Should I call her left wing or alt-right or, hell, should I just use whatever prefix she prefers or indeed none at all?

So it's not about how you stand then? No, she said, it's about safe space. According to my friend there have been extremely nasty arguments on Twitter where transgender women have threatened to whip out their penises and use them against TERF women. Now quite apart from the very real possibility that this has been a sarcastic quip, albeit a tasteless one, if it was serious this person should not be seen as representative of a group of transgender women but a troll, possibly a hate speech perpetrator or even a dangerous individual.

This dangerousness is not related to his or her gender whether born or chosen. The fact is, that this person's crime was not being transgender but being a twat of the highest order or even a criminal and should probably be taken out of circulation.

There are always a few in every group and their behaviour doesn't identify the whole group. In a Venn diagram of interlocking friends of the LBGTQ community, I'm in the 'don't sweat the small stuff' category. In just this way I believe anyone who wants to use the word woman to describe themselves should be able to. It in no way takes anything from those who never struggled with identity issues. Although I would hazard a guess that those who vehemently oppose it have issues of their own. Maybe, like my friend, very deep seated and understandable ones about male sexual domination, but which have nothing to do with whether Jim is simply happier and more comfortable being Jane or vice versa.

Then my friend plays her twat card with a word I've never come across before. And so I've just had to look up the word autogynephilia. This is what I don't get. In what way does that private fetish threaten women and womankind? If I get turned on by referring to myself as a sexy little camembert, how does that threaten the whole of cheesedom?

For me this question remains open as this problem of being happier with 100% female medics for gynae exams is one I do understand. As far as any other behaviour or misbehaviour by people who wish to be identified as female: the problem is not their gender. If they are twats they are simply twats and nothing else. If their behaviour is threatening or illegal then it should be treated as a criminal and not a gender issue.

So back to the right to use the word 'woman' which seems to be the crux of my friend's argument. My friend suggests that if the word 'woman' is stolen, there is now no separate word for her. And since she rejects any additions to it such as cisgender... fair enough, no need to use it. I have a suggestion for her and any woman who has this problem. There's a perfectly good word they can use to refer to themselves and it's... 'woman'. Why is that not enough? I have no interest in using stupid expressions like "People with wombs". Having had my own giblets thoroughly exenterated in a gloriously successful attempt to save my life. Having no womb left didn't suddenly switch me into any other category... apart maybe from the one in which I happily embrace the state of not having hormonal ups and downs. Being hormonally a woman is just so overrated!

Just as people have the right to have other clarifying adjectives to add to 'person' such as Malaysian, Christian and moustached, equally it's our right not to use excessive adjectives and simply describe ourselves as what we are or what we feel ourselves to be. My friend is the one who needs clarification to her description of herself so perhaps she might use 'transphobic' or just simply androphobic, which I completely understand especially in the case of people who have suffered abuse at the hands of men. To put this on all men and particularly those who do not wish to be part of that group really means your own misandry has become abusive in itself.

#197 Dicks.

Personally I think those who choose to identify as female and yet who literally wave their dicks around are twats of the highest order who actually damage the cause they pretend to espouse.

And finally

#198 Judgementalists twats.

Yes that's me, and perhaps all of us.

We are all judging and being judged all our lives. It seems we all need to garner as much love as possible or failing that, empathy or sympathy. We don't know what will fill that 'hole'.

One thing that helped me on my path towards finally understanding myself was reading my dad's memoir and finding out he was a human being. I had sort of realised that when he was frail and I was strong but I didn't look at him with the empathy I now can. In my eyes my dad was the most judgemental of all. He was intolerably racist in the way the middle class or aspiring middle class in our case, of that generation invariably were. When I heard Meghan Markle describe the discussion about her child's colour I both empathised and pooh poohed it because I'd had a similar discussion with my son about his own child, albeit in an excited grandma-to-be and wholly non race conscious way.

And looking further back I heard that my racist father had had that discussion several times with my mother and my elder brother. The fact that the discussion had taken place bothered me a lot less than that my brother seemed to need to repeat this to me ad-nauseam too. That was how my dad was. That was how old people were.

Yes he was a racist. There is no real 'but' is there? I could compare him to other people who were more racist and suggest the mildness of his sin and I would have people on both sides of the argument jumping on it, delighted to have yet one more situation to judge.

What I realised is that we are all juggling labels and judgements about people's culture, colour, financial situation, gender, sexual preference etc. ad-nauseam too. We're doing it because we need to be validated. We need in fact to have excuses for why we are both less than we want to be, and the other person is 'even worse'.

Anyway, reading his memoir I found that my father was just as rash and impulsive as I. Just as careless with money. Just as selfish at times and selfless at others. I also found that he had that fear of being judged. He came from a time and a class that were acutely aware that class structure was fragile and that at any time the house of glass could come tumbling down. Ahh. Not so different from now. If anything we are building more reasons to judge others as not OK, in order to feel more certain in an increasingly uncertain world.

The End... or the beginning.

Quite a lot of the topics within these pages touch on politics because all of life is politics. Whether you believe that or not you are affected every day by politics. So I've stopped there and shuffled a huge chunk of this book forward into a new document.

In the end, don't take my or anyone's judgements too seriously. We are all judgementalists, whether we're honest about it or not. Let's just learn to judge each other kindly and with affection, whenever possible.

I'd love to continue and put out the politics one which is likely to have even more people hopping up and down! The more feedback I get the more likely this is. Please let me know, and review if you enjoyed this book. And even if you didn't. Please back up your rating by comments. These are useful to me and informative to other readers. Of course authors depend on ratings and reviews so I really would appreciate yours.

Post script. *For those counting the actual number of twats featured in this book… congratulations. You have just outed yourself as number **#199**, although there are several others who were sub-categorised and didn't even get into the count.*

Biog

LittleOldLadyWho is the snarky-old-lady side of me… an otherwise tranquil 67 year old craft author. I live in Andalucia with my slightly (he would say a lot) younger husband and two feline fluff-monsters. We all enjoy cultivating the garden but we wish two of us wouldn't. We're mostly off grid and for the first time in our lives feel pretty free. We're not free of the thought that most people don't have that, and that things are getting worse.

My previous book, The Frugalist gets Amazon's 'Great on Kindle' label and has been well received for its gentle humour, clever frugal and sustainable hacks and a serious take on poverty.

My next book (I hope) will address the more difficult to laugh at, political twattery, which I took out of this one. It's more tricky to find any of that remotely funny. But I will try.

Thanks

To my Patreon patrons for support in my writing journey. I would never have been able to give any of my writing projects any time without you and I am incredibly grateful. I'm not going to 'out' you in this controversial book but you know who you are!

Thanks also to friends and family for providing a significant percentage of the twattery. Some in your actions, and more from your own irritation stories.

All characters in this book are purely fictional… except when they aren't.

My other Littleoldladywho books

The Frugalist

I was never prepared to swap too many of my hours for stuff. Hours are far too valuable a commodity to give up for stuff we don't want or need. Sometimes we want and use too much, and we take more from the planet than we can really appreciate. We waste valuable hours and give up our power in the process of getting more stuff.

Whether its time for an overhaul, or you just want the inspiration to make a few small changes, you will enjoy this book - you might even need some of it.

Bladder Cancer Stories

A cancer diagnosis challenges and changes you and the people who care for you in very many ways. Strangely, not all of them are bad.

I don't believe you are powerless in the face of even the most devastating news. We are all going to die, that's for sure, but like almost everyone, I'm dedicated to holding that day off as long as possible.

This is my story from a desperate search for answers through diagnosis, Radical Cystectomy and Chemotherapy. It's a story with a happy ending because I'm here to write it nearly 7 years later.

www.ingramcontent.com/pod-product-compliance
Lightning Source LLC
LaVergne TN
LVHW061548070526
838199LV00077B/6956